Feng Shui
Secrets

Improving Health, Wealth
& Relationship Harmony

The Feng Shui Checklist Worksheets

Can Be Found on Pages 19–24

———————————————

Photocopy These Pages for Each House You Plan to Evaluate,

or Download Additional Copies of the

Feng Shui Checklist Worksheets at:

www.ElliotTanzer.com

Feng Shui
Secrets

Improving Health, Wealth

& Relationship Harmony

Elliot Jay Tanzer

Do Your Own Feng Shui
Using the Feng Shui Checklist

PRINTED IN THE UNITED STATES of AMERICA

Previous Title: *Choose the Best House for You: The Feng Shui Checklist™*
First Printing - December 2003
Second Printing - September 2005
Revised Edition: *Feng Shui Secrets: Improving Health, Wealth & Relationship Harmony*
First Printing - August 2012

ISBN # 978-0-9743008-4-9
Library of Congress Control Number: 2012914137

Published by:

Elliot Jay Tanzer

P. O. Box 891924, Temecula, CA 92589-1924

☯

To order additional copies of
Feng Shui Secrets: Improving Health, Wealth & Relationship Harmony –
Do Your Own Feng Shui Using the Feng Shui Checklist™ call:
(310) 281-6798, or order on-line: www.ElliotTanzer.com

~ Acknowledgments ~

I have been fortunate to receive the teachings of feng shui from grandmasters, masters and those who some day will be masters and grandmasters. To all of these individuals I am greatly indebted. But first and foremost I am indebted to my friend James Allyn Moser, former CEO of the Feng Shui Warehouse. His encouragement to begin my training and the thoroughness of the Five-Day Practitioner's Training he, and fellow practitioner, Seann Xenja presented provided me with a solid foundation.

James, as a promoter and the convenor of four International Feng Shui Conferences, has also given me the opportunity to further my studies of Black Sect Tantric Buddhist Feng Shui with Grandmaster Prof. Lin Yun, and to tap the wealth of information regarding the use of the Luo P'an and the application of Eight Mansion and Flying Star Feng Shui formulas with Grandmaster Yap Cheng Hai, Master Raymond Lo, and many others including Prof. Jes T. Lim, David Twicken and Lillian Too.

I also have great appreciation for the remarkable lineage of teachers who have preserved and perpetuated feng shui teachings from their origins through many centuries of refinement. With this in mind I wish to acknowledge my deep gratitude to all my teachers who have assisted me throughout my life especially my first teachers, my parents, David and Pauline, and my brother Michael.

I also want to acknowledge my son Rama for his refinements to the cover art, his creative design for the Feng Shui Master Formula™ Study Guides, and his skill as webmaster in designing my website: www.ElliotTanzer.com. And a special thanks for editorial support from Joan Wilcox, Karen Stover, Leigh Christian, and Laurei Southam.

And of course I am thankful for the loving support of my youngest son, Andrew, and lovely lady Holly.

My life has been truly blessed a thousand fold,

Elliot

Temecula, CA
October 2003

Contents

A Note on Why "Qi" and Not "Ch'i," "Chi" or "Chee"   6

Your First Steps to Good Feng Shui

Guidelines to Energy Flow Analysis: What Is Qi and How Qi Flows   9

Examples of Qi Flow: Basis for Questions on the Feng Shui Checklist   14

The Feng Shui Checklist Procedure: How to Use This Book   15

The Feng Shui Checklist Worksheets: the Questions   19

Influences of the External Environment

House Problems With No Solutions: Houses to Avoid   27

Gathering Clues About a Home's Feng Shui: Law of the Predecessors   33

The First Criteria: Does It Meet Your Needs?   37

The Ideal House Site: Evaluating the Property   39

Neighbors – Harmony in the Community   57

Interior Harmony

House Structure: How Energy Flows Through the Home   65

Attracting Opportunities: Evaluating the Entrance   83

Rest, Rejuvenation, and Romance: Evaluating the Bedroom   99

Other Rooms to Consider: Kitchen, Dining Room, Child's Room,

Home Office, and Garage   113

Additional Feng Shui Secrets – Ancient & Modern

Wealth and Partnership Areas of the Home: the 3-Door Bagua Template   125

Things to Change If You Can: Removing Contributors to Poor Feng Shui   135

Things to Fix Immediately: Keeping the Home in Good Condition   139

Change Your Location, Change Your Life: Global Feng Shui   143

Exploring Other Ways to Feng Shui Your Home   147

Bibliography: Other Books to Further Your Study of Feng Shui   150

About the Author, Speaker Availability, Product, and Services   151

Note on Why "Qi" and Not "Ch'i," "Chi" or "Chee"

When qi is carried by the wind, it is dispersed;
when it comes to the water, it is accumulated.
~~ Master Guo Pu [276-324CE], The Zangshu, or Book of Burial

From the mid-19th Century until 1958, the attempt to transliterate the many characters of the Chinese language into the Roman alphabet of the Occident was known as the Wade-Giles system. With the success of Chairman Mao and the Communist Party's takeover of the Chinese mainland, in an attempt to unify a nation of many traditional dialects and languages, the Mandarin language/dialect was mandated as the one to be used by all citizens of the new China.

Along with this attempt to create a nationwide homogenization, was the development of a new system of Romanization called Pinyin. It is this Pinyin system that has since become the recognized official national standard for transcribing Chinese characters into the Roman alphabet. By 1982, it was accepted as the international standard, and then Taiwan, the last holdout, finally adopted it as recently as 2009.

The attempt to adapt it to a variety of Occidental languages, as diverse as English, French, and the Cyrillic Script of eastern European countries, has resulted in some strange results. This is especially evident in the transliteration of the words which are the primary subject of this book. In the West these words are phonetically pronounce as "füng sch'way" and "chee."

In the Wade-Giles system, the Chinese word sounding like "chee" was transliterated as *ch'i* (the apostrophe is inserted after a consonantal aspiration before a syllable starting with a vowel, as in *ch*eek or *ch*in). This is often mistakenly written as *chi* (by those who do not understand the use of the apostrophe to indicate a consonantal aspiration, and discarded as extraneous).

While *ch'i* in the Wade-Giles system is close to the phonetic spelling of "chee", the Pinyin version of *ch'i* is totally different, and, as it is spelled *qi,* can even be considered bizarre. As far as my research has unearthed, this strange decision to transliterate the *ch'* as the letter "q" has something to do with accommodating the problems of transcribing this letter sound into the Armenian language. For the record, the *ch* in *chi* without an apostrophe after it, signifies a flat tone, and should be pronounced and transcribed in Pinyin as *zh*, as in the 'j' in *j*unk or 'ch' in *ch*oke. It is found in older writings as *Chen*, the name of one of the eight Trigrams in Wade-Giles, while in modern Pinyin is now written as *Zhen* Trigram.

In the first printing of this book, under the title of *Choose the Best House for You: The Feng Shui Checklist*, I resisted the accepted modern spelling, and went with *ch'i,* as the spelling that was the most visually similar to the phonetic "chee," and which had the longest history of use, and therefore, of familiarity. However, with the new book title, revisions, and added material, I decided to surrender my attachment to the visually logical, and take this opportunity to explain to you why I have decided to use the modern spelling of *qi*; and why, in the various quotes from other authors sprinkled around the book, I have retained the spelling as the author of the quote wrote it, whether ch'i, chi, qi, feng shui, Feng Shui, or the hyphenated feng-shui. In fact, my original working title for this book was, *Let the Qi Flow*. And indeed, that's what it's really all about.

Your First Step to Good Feng Shui

Everything is Integral to Everything Else

The influence of the natural configuration of the ground
is very powerful in its influence upon the destiny of man,
but man may alter the natural configurations,
and improve the aspects of any unfavorable locality.
We see, therefore, it is left in a great measure to man's foresight and energy
to turn his fortunes into any channel he pleases,
to modify and regulate the influences which heaven and earth bring to bear upon him
and it is the boast of the Feng-shui system that it teaches man
how to rule nature and his own destiny by showing him how heaven and earth rule him.
~~ Ernest J. Eitel,
Feng Shui: The Science of Sacred Landscape in Old China

Health, Wealth &
Great Good Fortune

Guidelines to Energy Flow Analysis

What is Qi and How Qi Flows

Feng he, ri li, shui qing, shu mao.
Mild wind, warm sun, clear water, lush vegetation,
the essential ingredients for a site with good feng shui.

~~ H.H. Prof. Thomas Lin Yun

In this book, you will learn to use the most basic feng shui principles and methods to evaluate the energy of your property, your neighborhood, how your home is designed, and how the rooms are configured. You will learn to identify how the energy flows to, through and around your home, and which areas have beneficial feng shui. Areas with feng shui that can be detrimental will also be identified with suggestions about how to transform this potentially negative energy flow so it can become beneficial.

Searching for a Home with Good Feng Shui

The Feng Shui Checklist actually began when a student asked, "I'm house hunting. Do you have any feng shui guidelines?" I said, "sure," and typed up a one page list. The Feng Shui Checklist on the following pages also grew out of my own family's search for a good feng shui home. In our search, we looked at many homes and noted their many problems. Many of these problems and solutions were added to the original list of feng shui guidelines.

The one page list soon grew to the 166 questions that comprise the Feng Shui Checklist found on pages 19 to 24, making this the most comprehensive list of energy flow problems compiled anywhere. As these problems and solutions were added, they were also being organized and re-organized according to different categories as listed in the Contents. This invaluable resource of feng shui problems and their solutions focuses on the physical reality of a house: the energy of the property, the energy of the home in relationship to its surroundings, and the energy of how the home was constructed.

What Is Qi?

Qi is the Chinese word for "energy." Everything animate and inanimate, real or conceptual, has qi. Different people have different qi. Each kind of animal has its own kind of qi. A nation has its qi and a religion has its qi. There is roadway qi, rock qi, locational qi, and vocational qi. There is soft-yin qi and hard-yang qi. There is children qi, male and female qi. Each item of food has its unique qi. To identify the qi of anything animate or inanimate, real or conceptual, is to understand its essential nature. Qi is the *Isness* of whatever is – the essence of the thing or situation. If your goal is good health and success in all areas of your life, there is no other concept more important than the study and understanding of qi, and how qi flows.

Ch'i is the nonbiological self – our spirit, our psyche, our essence.
~~ Sara Rossbach, *Interior Design with Feng Shui*

Why Feng Shui

The study of how qi in our working and living environments affects us is called feng shui (füng sch'way). The art and science of feng shui is based on many thousands of years of observation and application. Knowing the feng shui of how our environment affects us allows us to alter the qi flow to be more beneficial. Feng shui techniques allow us to mitigate the negative influences while enhancing the positive ones.

The Chinese words *feng* and *shui* are actually descriptions of qi flow. "Feng" means wind and "shui" means water. Feng, as wind, refers to the invisible or intangible qi that flows through a space. Shui, as water, is the visible, more tangible flow of qi. The study of feng shui encompasses all the ways that qi can have an effect on the inhabitants of any specific environment.

How Do You Know If You Have Good Feng Shui?

The answer is: Are you happy and healthy? Are you enjoying prosperity, or at least more than enough to provide for your needs? Do you have a good reputation? Do you have a committed, mutually supportive and satisfying personal relationship? Are your children thriving, respectful, and socially conscious? Are they creative and successful academically? If your answer is "yes" to each of these questions, then the answer to the original question is: "Yes, the house you are living in has good feng shui."

If your house does not have good feng shui for wealth, you are always running to catch up. If your house does not have good feng shui for health, you are often tired and stressed. If your house does not have good feng shui for relationship harmony, you are single (which in some cases might be a life style choice), or you are in an unhappy relationship, and might as well be living alone. If you have children and they are a source of ongoing concern, grief, and melodrama, and if so, it could be yet another indicator that your home has unfavorable feng shui.

Of course, the feng shui of your house may be just good enough, so that you are doing well in some of these areas, while not doing well in others; or, not doing well in one area may be distracting you from doing even better in all the others.

The Nature of Life-Giving, or Upward Moving Energy – Sheng Qi

All beneficial qi is pleasant, uplifting, and inspiring. It is anything that is pleasant to smell, hear, or look at. Beneficial qi flow is smooth, graceful, and its movement can be described as meandering. Meandering qi is nurishing and easy to accumulate. Anything that allows us to relax and encourages us to interact with others harmoniously reflects good qi and good qi flow. Good qi enables us to maintain concentration, productivity, and enthusiasm, as well as restful sleep, intimate relationships, and moments of quiet contemplation. Good qi flow attracts opportunity, and the awareness to take advantage of a good opportunity, when it comes our way. An environment that has

The Chinese philosopher Hsu said that ch'i comes from ling, which are tiny, airborne particles or molecular charges that circulate in the universe and enter the womb at conception. When we are born, ling becomes ch'i; when we die, our ch'i returns to the limitless universal ling.

~~ Jami Lin, ed.
The Feng Shui Anthology: Contemporary Earth Design

meandering qi flow is harmonious to live in. Everything in nature – including people – that is vibrant and joyous is an example of life-giving qi. Calm, meandering, pleasant qi is the standard against which all other qi can be measured. The Chinese words for life-giving qi is *sheng qi* – literally, "upward moving energy."

Sha Qi – Noxious Energy That Takes Life Away

When qi moves too fast, too slow, is excessive or deficient, is overbearing or distracting, or is in any way extreme, it is an example of *sha qi*. Sha qi is noxious, stress producing, and unhealthy. Sha qi undermines our vitality, focus, enthusiasm, and emotional equanimity. Sha qi is also referred to as "killing qi." It can be said with certainty that sha qi literally takes life away.

In evaluating a home we are currently living in, or in our search for a property and home design that supports a fulfilling life, we must be conscious of the environmental sources of unhealthy, sha qi. The important goal of a feng shui diagnosis, is not only to encourage good qi to accumulate, but also to identify the presence of sha qi and then consider ways to transform it to the more desirable and beneficial life-giving sheng qi.

Hidden Arrows – A Type of Sha Qi

In contrast to life-giving, smooth flowing, meandering qi, anything in nature that moves in a straight line is a form of sha qi. Sha qi that comes from straight lines, sharp and pointy edges or angles is called a "hidden arrow." Some call hidden arrows "poison arrows." Hidden arrows or poison arrows "shoot" qi rapidly in the direction the "arrow" is pointing.

The sha qi from "hidden arrows" are destructive. This can be seen when we compare a gently flowing stream to a rushing river. Such a fast moving river strips the trees from its banks. Or when we compare an animal peacefully foraging in a forest compared to a panicked animal crashing through the same forest breaking branches and trampling foliage underfoot. A straight line enables qi to flow too fast. The natural human response to a "hidden arrow," whether a flash flooding river or an animal raging out of control, is to get out of the way as quickly as possible. The need for security and feeling safe motivates many of the suggested feng shui solutions.

The presence of "hidden arrows" in the home elicits the same response of getting out of danger's way. For example: if you were seated in your dining room eating dinner and someone was standing in the corner pointing a bow and arrow at you, understandably you would be tense and nervous. You would ask them to put it down, or at least point it in a different direction. Even if instead of a live person, it was a statue of the beautiful huntress Diana with her bow and arrow carved out of wood or stone, you would still feel uneasy. Without too much hesitation you would soon get up, turn the statue, and point the arrow in a different direction – a direction away from you.

Ch'i travels in a curve. When it is forced into a straight line, it acts like a bullet from a gun or an arrow from a bow that threatens to wound anything at the receiving end. Feng Shui strives to protect a space or site from these secret arrows.

~~ Angel Thompson,
*The Feng Shui Anthology:
Contemporary Earth Design*

Some "hidden arrows" are quite obvious, while others are very abstract. They are embedded in the environment and are not clearly perceived as an actual arrow shaft with a life-threatening, sharp-pointed arrowhead. Consequently, many "hidden arrows" are often ignored by the conscious or rational mind.

Though ignored by the conscious (rational) mind, the subconscious (emotional) mind continues to squirm in its little understood attempt to get out of the way of danger – to get out of the "line of fire." People often sense something is wrong, but have difficulty identifying the problem. Presented with an angle of the wall, a sharp corner of furniture, or a pointy-leaf plant, the subconscious prepares for the inevitable impact of this "arrow," even though in reality, it will never fly forth. To the subconscious (emotional) mind there is no differentiation between the illusion of danger, and the dangerous situation that is real. The subconscious will do whatever is necessary to avoid danger without the more consciously aware rational mind necessarily being aware of what evasive action may have been set into motion.

How "Hidden Arrows" Undermine Health

This constant tensing in anticipation of being hit and hurt keeps the adrenal glands' 'fight and flight' response at high alert. Along with the adrenal glands secretion of adrenaline, the 'fight and flight' hormone, other symptoms of a body in tension are: accelerated heart beat, high blood pressure, and rapid and shallow breathing. If this tense posturing continues unabated for prolonged periods of time, day after day, year after year, the immune system is ultimately undermined and various health problems are likely to manifest. Acupuncturist call this Triple Warmer Meridian activation.

At the same time the immune system is weakening, the area of the body in direct line of the "hidden arrow" becomes inflamed. It eventually collapses when put under real pressure during sports or even normal everyday activities. The blame is quickly put on the activity instead of on the real culprit, the environmental presence of a "hidden arrow." Like all sha qi, "hidden arrows" need to be removed, blocked, or deflected.

Qi Flows In Many Ways – Landform Feng Shui

The first challenge of a feng shui diagnosis is to determine how qi flows to, through, and around the home, and then to identify if it is beneficial or detrimental. Beneficial qi flow can be enhanced and energized, or enjoyed just as it is. But it is of the utmost importance to identify the problem areas that are causing unfortunate sha qi. Once you identify the problem areas, your next challenge is to find solutions. Solutions that will regulate the qi flow to ensure that it flows smoothly and abundantly.

In nature, rivers, mountains, valleys, trees, meadows, pathways, and other landscape features are all channels for qi flow. In cities, this translates as roadways, alleyways, buildings, and open spaces. Inside a home, qi flows through an "internal landscape" of

When you are in good health, your metabolism and internal secretions function properly. Your chi is correctly aligned and you feel energetic and happy. This state regenerates itself and sustains health."

~~ Mark Mafori,
Feng Shui:
Discover Money, Health & Love

doors, windows, stairways, and hallways, and is assisted or blocked by furniture, appliances, design elements, and structural components of the house. As we have seen, when qi flow to, through, or around a home is obstructed, stagnant, or excessive, the health and well-being of the inhabitants are adversely affected. In contrast, smooth and abundant qi flow through the "outside and internal landscape" results in a sense of self-assurance and a more positive outlook – a sense of being in the flow.

Whether mountains or rivers outside or furniture and hallways inside, this approach is called Landform Feng Shui, and is the foundation upon which all other systems of feng shui depend on for their efficiency and long term effectiveness. As with all systems of feng shui, the goal of Landform Feng Shui is to attract, accumulate, and hold on to the good qi long enough to be enjoyed as a benefit, before it flows on again.

Landform Feng Shui
Heaven and Earth, mountains and valleys, and how the qi flows inside and outside.

Feng Shui to the Rescue – Working Smarter, Instead of Harder

Another useful metaphor for the home is its comparison to a bucket-like container – a container that holds energy. Imagine going to a well, filling your bucket to the brim, only to discover upon arriving home, the bucket was riddled with holes of various sizes, and is empty? If you are not aware the bucket has holes, you might run around frenetically trying to replace what was lost until collapsing from exhaustion.

Or, instead of racing madly around trying to keep a leaky container full, you can use the Feng Shui Checklist to identify the "energy leaks, and then cleverly "patch the holes." In this way subsequent trips to the well will be more successful. In short, by removing, blocking, or deflecting sha qi we make the container-like home stronger. Problem solving solutions are called remedies, cures, or countermeasures. Solutions to make a good situation even better are called enhancements or energizers.

Of course, if the identified sources of sha qi cannot be removed, blocked or deflected, as some sources of sha qi are more detrimental than others, a decision has to be made as to how serious the problem is? Once the problem has been identified, almost all situations can be easily remedied. In the worst case scenarios, the only solution is to pack up and move. The Feng Shui Checklist format of this book was designed to enable you to evaluate all the possible ways sha qi can be found in and around the home.

Creating Harmonious Qi Flow

Everything felt by our senses is evaluated by both the conscious (rational) mind as well as the subconscious (feeling) mind. It is a natural inclination for living things to be attracted to that which is soft, curvy, and accommodating, and to feel rebuffed or put off by that which is hard, angular, aggressive, and uninviting. By improving the household qi, you improve your own personal qi with more calm, equanimity and joy. By applying feng shui principles and methods, you will be able to create beneficial qi flow in the home, and enjoy a happy and harmonious life.

Remedies are also called cures, and can be ch'i activators, adjusters, enhancers, stimulators, lifters, stabilizers, or deflectors, depending upon the correction needed. When placing feng shui remedies, it is especially important to remember that they are to be put in place with a sincere heart while setting a clear intention.

~~ Holly Ziegler,
Sell Your Home FASTER with Feng Shui: Ancient Wisdom to Expedite the Sale of Real Estate

Examples of Qi Flow

The Basis for the Questions on the Feng Shui Checklist

Life-Giving, or Upward Moving (Sheng) Qi – Qi Flow Which Can Be Enhanced

• **Meandering qi** – moves along casually and gracefully. It is qi that is the most nourishing and easiest to accumulate. It encourages focus and stability, and translates as a natural rhythm. Meandering qi leads to harmony, which expresses itself as good health, prosperity, and nurturing relationships. It is pleasant, calming, and enjoyable. Meandering qi signifies the ideal. The qi of all things can be evaluated and compared to this standard.

• **Expansive qi** – is open, light and gives a feeling of spaciousness and comfort.

• **Positive symbolic qi** – is found in images, items, or certain patterns that are psychologically uplifting, inspiring, and motivating.

Forms of Sha Qi – Qi That Needs to Be Adjusted

Sha qi is detrimental. Most feng shui solutions are designed to prevent sha qi and increase good, sheng qi. Sha qi can express itself in any of the following ways:

• **Fast moving qi** – needs to be slowed down. Fast moving qi from long hallways and heavily trafficked roadways can over-energize the adrenal glands and leads to physical fatigue.

• **Excessive qi** – needs to be diffused. Excessive qi from large windows and found in large spaces is over-stimulating and leads to loss of focus and nervous exhaustion.

• **Obstructed qi** – needs to be unblocked. Obstructed qi from clutter, blank walls, and poorly positioned furniture causes frustration and leads to stress, anxiety, and inertia.

• **Stagnant qi** – needs to be freshened. Stagnant qi from standing water or poor ventilation is unhealthy, devitalizing, and leads to depression and poor health.

• **Compressed qi** – needs to be redirected. Compressed qi from overhead beams or slanted ceilings inflames the area of the body "under pressure," making it vulnerable to injury and illness.

• **Chopping qi** – needs to be deflected or diffused. Chopping qi from overhead fans generate fear and uncertainty. Ceiling fans directly above the head disturb the heart and nervous system.

• **Split qi** – needs to be unified. Split qi from pillars and structural supports is disorienting and leads to confusion, misunderstanding, arguments, and indecisiveness.

• **Excessive yin qi** – needs to be dried out and warmed up. Excessive yin qi from too much water, lush foliage, or dark shadows encourages mold growth and poor air quality and leads to problems of the urinary tract, kidneys, and lymphatic system.

• **Excessive yang qi** – needs to be moistened and cooled down. Excessive yang qi from too much heat or bright lights leads to frantic activity, over heating, and dehydration. This can stress the heart, raises the blood pressure, dries the kidneys, and exhausts the adrenal glands.

• **Negative symbolic qi** – is found in images, items, or certain patterns which have negative associations with death, divorce, sickness, fears, painful situations or memories, and so on. Negative symbols need to be removed, as they can result in depression, anxiety, relationship disharmony, and ill-health. Only use symbolic qi that is positive and uplifting.

The Feng Shui Checklist Procedure

How to Use This Book

We shape our dwellings, and afterwards
our dwellings shape us.
~~ Sir Winston Churchill

The Feng Shui Checklist will help you to easily and quickly make an accurate and comprehensive evaluation of any home you are considering buying, renting, or are currently living in. In just a short time you will know about the positive qi aspects of the house and its property, and about the negative qi aspects. When you discover sha qi – qi that could create disharmony – you will learn how to correct the problem to get positive sheng qi flowing again. You might also discover that some problems have no acceptable solutions. If there are many unsolvable qi problems, either avoid buying or renting such a home, or if you are already reside in such a dwelling, consider moving on, until you find a home with a more positive feng shui foundation.

A Strong Feng Shui Foundation

With a strong feng shui foundation your home will provide you with the maximum security and support in all your endeavors from restful regenerative sleep to intimate romantic interludes; from inspiration and success in all your projects to academic achievement for your children. In short, whatever you imagine your best life to be, choosing a home with a strong feng shui foundation will ensure that you will be supported during the inevitable ups and downs that come with our relatively brief stay on planet Earth. A strong feng shui foundation is also necessary for all other more advanced feng shui techniques, as taught by other feng shui schools, to be effective.

My Suggestion

If you are evaluating the home you are currently living in, and if you are planning to evaluate the homes of family and friends, I would suggest you photocopy the Feng Shui Checklist Worksheets on pages 19 through 24; or, go to my website, www.ElliotTanzer.com, where you will be able to Download and print out as many additional copies you may need. If you are house hunting, you may want to make several photocopies in preparation of looking at many homes before deciding on the one that is best for you. Write the address of the house under consideration in the space provided. This will help you keep an accurate record of each house you evaluate.

It is also suggested that you obtain accurate floor plans or at least a fairly accurate sketch, so you can get a better overview of the layout of the house, the room configurations, connecting hallways, and the relationship of doors, windows, and even toilets in regard to their effect on frequently used areas of the home. A good floor plan, along with a stack of photographs, is also what you will need to send me, if you want my assistance in helping you to make your final decision.

Perfect Feng Shui? Not Likely

Drawing from the different levels of feng shui evaluation, we should consider ourselves lucky if we can find a home that has at least 70% good feng shui to begin with. Then, by applying the various feng shui techniques of qi adjustment, we can attempt to resolve as many of the remaining 30% of feng shui problems as we could. Outside the home qi adjustments can often be made by landscaping, or if necessary by remodeling. Inside the home qi adjustments can be accomplished by decorating and also if necessary by remodeling. In my next book, *Feng Shui Interior Design Secrets*, I will describe ways to use furniture and decorations to enhance beneficial qi, and which design elements to avoid.

Though there are a few extreme situations that make a home totally uninhabitable (House Problems With No Solutions, page 27), the vast majority of feng shui problems listed in the Feng Shui Checklist can be easily remedied. With each feng shui problem listed I do my best to provide you with the parameters to guide you in making a correct evaluation of how serious the problem may be, and how to apply the appropriate remedy. When in doubt, call an experienced feng shui practitioner. Or go to my website, www.ElliotTanzer.com, click "Contact," and then send me an email with your questions.

Using the Feng Shui Checklist to Discover Problems
& Determine Solutions

Our first concern is to reveal the problems inherent in the dwelling. Our next concern is to determine if the identified problem is resolvable; and, if so, what degree of effort will be be required to resolve such a problem and whether or not it will be worth the effort?

The questions listed in the Feng Shui Checklist are mostly examples of feng shui problems that can be found in and around the home environment. Some of the questions are phrased in the negative in order to keep all the "yes" answers consistent. As we are mostly concerned with locating problems that need to be remedied, read through the questions of the Feng Shui Checklist and make a ☑ in the first row of boxes only if there is a PROBLEM, and **leave the box blank if there is no problem**. Making a check mark only for problems will also help to keep the worksheets uncluttered as you go back to review the problems and consider the solutions.

After you have answered all the questions, go back over your list and review the problems of the house by reading the page numbers provided at the end of each question. Here you will find a description and illustration of each problem in greater detail, why it is a problem, and how to evaluate the severity of the problem. After reading the description of the problem, the next paragraph will give solutions. Here you will find suggestions on how to alter the detrimental nature of the problem, and how to transform it into more positive, harmonious qi flow. As some feng shui terminology may be new to you, or to clarify the questions, it may be necessary to first read the description on the page given for a specific question in order to determine if the problem does apply to you, and to understand how to make an accurate assessment.

After reading the solutions given for those question you had ☑'ed in the first row of boxes, record if the problem can be easily resolved in the second row of boxes. If the problem CANNOT be remedied,

☑ the box to indicate the problem still remains. If the problem noted can be resolved and is no longer to be considered as a problem, leave the box unmarked. This way, if you decide to choose this house to live in, you can go back to the checklist to review the problem and determine which solutions to apply.

Once you have answered all the questions and reviewed all the solutions, you can evaluate the degree of severity any of the difficult to remedy feng shui flaws are likely to have on your life. And remember, all the situations mentioned in this book are meant as guidelines. Real life situations may vary and require you to adapt what you have read. One size does not necessarily fit all. Ultimately, you may have to trust your intuition, or seek assistance from a trained feng shui practitioner.

As I know from personal experience, searching for a home with good feng shui can at times be frustrating. Be patient and don't panic. Remember, 100% good feng shui is not probable, so don't become obsessed trying to find a "perfect" feng shui home. From a feng shui point-of-view all homes have problems. Your challenge is to find the home with the best feng shui possible, identify the potential problems, consider the suggested remedies, and to remain calm in the process. Consider each prospective house carefully, and then choose the best home for you and your family.

Feng – Wind

Shui – Water

THE FENG SHUI CHECKLIST
PROCEDURE SUMMARIZED

Before You Begin

1. Photocopy the Feng Shui Checklist printed on the next five pages, or go to www.ElliotTanzer.com to Download and print additional copies, so you can use the Feng Shui Checklist for yourself or for your family and friends.

2. Though most of the evaluation will be done as you walk through a home you are currently living in or considering to buy or rent, if possible, obtain an accurate architect's floor plan of the home you are evaluating, or at least a fairly accurate hand-drawn sketch, showing the rooms of the house, how they relate to each other, and any unusual configurations. Having an actual floor plan may assist you in discovering what is located in the center of the home, where toilets are situated, and many other factors that may not be easily identified during your walk through of the home you are evaluating.

Using the Feng Shui Checklist Worksheets

1. Answer the first eight questions: House Problems With No Solutions. If you ☑'ed any of these questions indicating one of these problems does apply to the house in question, avoid this house and look for another.

2. The next six questions pertain to the Law of Predecessors, which states that whatever happened to the previous occupants will probably happen to all future occupants. If you can determine what happened to the previous owners or tenants, you may have clues as to what feng shui problems the home has, and what you will need to do to remedy the situation before it becomes your problem as well.

3. The remaining 154 questions will determine if your home has at least 70% good feng shui. Only ☑ boxes in the first row (**Before** column), if a problem applies. Leave the box empty if there is no problem. The first questions are subjective in nature. The First Criteria are: Does the house conform with your basic priorities of price, size, location and your family's life-style choices? And does it feel good? Your home is a reflection of you. If you are not content with your home, your unhappiness and discomfort will undermine your personal qi.

4. Now you are ready to walk around the outside of the house and answer the questions regarding the influence the external environment has on the home.

5. Then walk through the house and answer the questions regarding the influence of the internal structure and room configurations. Pay special attention to your evaluation of the entrance and the bedroom. In fact, after evaluating the entrance, consider going straight to the bedroom next. Answering the questions beginning on page 99, determine how the bed will be positioned. If the bedroom has no major problems and is acceptable, then continue to evaluate other rooms and features of the home. If the bedroom has major problems, leave.

6. Finally, consider the questions in Section III: Additional Feng Shui Secrets.

Determining A Home's Feng Shui

1. When you have read all the solutions to the ☑'ed boxes on the Feng Shui Checklist Worksheets you will have a clear idea of what problems the house might have. You are now ready to read the page numbers provided with each question you ☑'ed to determine if the discovered problem is easy or difficult to resolve.

2. In the second row of boxes (**After** column), if the problem can be resolved, leave the box empty so you know the problem has a Solution listed. Only ☑ a box in the second row if the problem is difficult or cannot be solved.

3. Before making a final decision, review the ☑'ed boxes in the first column and those with both rows of boxes ☑'ed, consider how many problems there are, their possible consequences, their solutions if any, and then determine if the home is the best choice for you and your family.

The *Feng Shui Secrets*
Feng Shui Checklist™

**Worksheets for evaluating a house you are planning
to buy, rent, or are currently living in.**

by Elliot Jay Tanzer

HOUSE ADDRESS: _____

(Photocopy this Checklist to separately evaluate each home or apartment you are examining,
or go to www.ElliotTanzer.com to Download and print out as many copies as needed.)

House Problems With No Solutions

Read the following eight questions. If you place a ☑ to any of these questions – DO NOT go further. The house under consideration will bring misfortune. If there are no to these first eight questions, continue answering the questions that follow. If you need help answering any questions, turn to the page number provided and read the full description of the problem listed.

Before After

NO CURES

❏   1. Extremely odd-shaped houses lacking a clear center: crescent-shaped, extreme modular, etc. Page 27

❏   2. Property on reclaimed wetlands or former garbage dumping site. Page 28

❏   3. Property on a cemetery or ancient burial grounds. Page 28

❏   4. Houses built on the edge of a cliff, ravine, or gulch. Page 29

❏   5. Houses built at the bottom of a canyon wall, or under a rock overhang, freeway or railroad overpass – "tiger's jaws." Page 29

❏   6. Fast moving river, rainwater drainage ditch, or roadway directly behind or in front of the house. Page 30

❏   7. Houses with excessive outside noises, obnoxious smells or toxic fumes. Page 30

❏   8. Houses close to a utility pole transformer, power generator station or substation, high tension wires, microwave dish, airport radar, or a nuclear power plant. Page 31

Gathering Clues About a Home's Feng Shui

If you are dealing with a real estate agent or landlord, the answers to the following four questions should be easy to obtain. If you have the opportunity to meet the previous owners or tenants, do not be shy about asking about their life. **Mark a ☑ in the box if any of these problems exist.** In order to change its feng shui, you will need to find the cause of each problem that is found. You will be able to determine if the problem(s) can be remedied, after you answer the remaining questions in the Feng Shui Checklist and determine what caused these problems to come to pass. **If a problem cannot be remedied, ☑ the box in the second row of boxes.** Even if you can remedy the problem, it is still advisable to clear the previous owner's or tenant's energy by doing a Space Clearing as described on page 33.

Before After

❏ ❏ 9. Were the previous owners financially successful? After this house did they move up in life to a better situation (leave box blank)? or did they have financial problems and move down (☑ in box)? Page 35

❏ ❏ 10. Did the previous owners or tenants have relationship problems? Page 35

❏ ❏ 11. Did the previous owners or tenants have serious health problems? Page 35

❏ ❏ 12. Did the previous owners or tenants have other major problems to consider? Page 35

The First Criteria: Does It Meet Your Needs

The answers to the next six questions are subjective and need to be considered. Finances or other factors may dictate that the home under consideration cannot satisfy your personal requirements. If you cannot satisfy your personal needs, it is important to satisfy as many of the other requirements of good feng shui in order to increase your prosperity, or change whatever circumstance is keeping you from choosing a home you are emotionally comfortable in, so you can improve your situation as soon as possible. There are no cures for these situations other than to make do, and move into a home more to your liking as soon as you are able.

Before After

NO CURES

❑ 13. Does it feel good – do you like the appearance, neighborhood, views, or whatever makes a place feel like home to you? Page 37

❑ 14. Does it offer enough space for you (and your family's) current needs? Page 37

❑ 15. Will it satisfy your changing needs (and those of your family as your family grows)? Page 37

❑ 16. Is it in proximity to work? Page 37

❑ 17. Does it feel safe and will it provide the opportunity for peaceful, rejuvenating sleep? Page 37

❑ 18. If there are children, is it easy for them to get to school and after school activities without adding stressful demands on the parents? Page 37

The Ideal House Site: Evaluating the Property

All the following questions should be self explanatory. They are all problems that need to be solved. Some are worded in the negative to be consistent in receiving a ☑ if the answer is "Yes, there is a Problem," or leave blank if there is no problem. After answering all the questions, read the page number after each question you marked with a ☑ to determine why it is a problem, how serious the problem is, and what the solution(s) might be. If the problem CANNOT be easily remedied, ☑ the box in the second row of boxes. If the problem can be remedied, leave the box in the second row of boxes unchecked to indicate it is no longer a problem but that you will want to review the solutions later if you choose to rent or buy this home. Now reread the ☑s to be sure the remaining problems are not severe. Note: It may be necessary to turn to the page number provided to read the problem descriptions before attempting to answer some questions (ex.: #19 and #20, and any other questions where descriptions are not clear to you).

Before After

❑ ❑ 19. Is the house NOT surrounded by the "four celestial animals" to form an "armchair" configuration? Page 39

❑ ❑ 20. Are the "azure dragon" and the "white tiger" NOT in proper balance? Page 40

❑ ❑ 21. Is the house built on a mountain top – on a "dragon's head, back or tail?" Page 42

❑ ❑ 22. Is there poor soil quality and lack of greenery? Page 42

❑ ❑ 23. Does the property look like a triangle, rhomboid or other irregular shape (not a square or rectangle)? Page 43

❑ ❑ 24. Is the house situated on the front, middle or back third of the property? Page 45

❑ ❑ 25. Is the house built too close to the ocean surf or body of water? Page 46

❑ ❑ 26. Are there mountains or very large buildings close behind or to either side? Page 46

❑ ❑ 27. Is the house on the end of a dead-end street or a cul-de-sac? Page 46

❑ ❑ 28. Is the house located on outer edge of a river, roadway, curving highway overpass, or busy corner lot? Page 48

❑ ❑ 29. Is the house attacked by "tiger eyes" (headlights) at night? Page 49

❑ ❑ 30. Is the house on a T-intersection or Y-intersection? Page 49

❑ ❑ 31. Is the house on a road without a curb or step up to the front door? Page 50

❑ ❑ 32. Is the house or apartment down steps below street level? Page 50

❑ ❑ 33. Is the house down hill from a roadway? Page 50

Before After

❏ ❏ 34. Is the house at the bottom of a steep road or driveway – an "uphill struggle?" Page 51

❏ ❏ 35. Is the house at the top of a steep road or driveway – "opportunities roll away?" Page 51

❏ ❏ 36. Is the house on a one way street? Page 52

❏ ❏ 37. Are cars parked pointing directly at the entrance, bedroom or other frequently used rooms? Page 52

❏ ❏ 38. Are there high walls or foliage, so the roof of the house is hidden from the street? Page 53

❏ ❏ 39. Do frequently used rooms face predominantly west? Page 53

❏ ❏ 40. Do frequently used rooms face predominantly north? Page 54

❏ ❏ 41. Is there a pond in the back yard, or to the right of the front door? Page 54

❏ ❏ 42. Is there a swimming pool? What is its shape? How is it positioned? Page 55

❏ ❏ 43. Is there a geopathic stress zone running under the house – the "Claws of the Dragon.?" Page 55

Neighbors: Harmony in the Community

❏ ❏ 44. Do the neighboring houses "attack" each other with sharp corners, gables, or rooftop edges? Page 58

❏ ❏ 45. Is there a "tiger's mouth" opposite your front door – "big door eats little door?" Page 58

❏ ❏ 46. Is your neighbor's driveway and garage door opposite your front door? Page 59

❏ ❏ 47. Is there a house on the same property uphill from the house you are considering? Page 59

❏ ❏ 48. Are there neighboring houses higher up a hill? Page 59

❏ ❏ 49. Are there disagreeable or disturbing neighbors? Page 60

❏ ❏ 50. Is the house in view of a cemetery, house of worship, hospital, mortuary, or slaughter house? Page 60

❏ ❏ 51. Can you see church crosses, factory smoke stacks, a quarry, waste water reclamation, etc? Page 60

House Structure: How Energy Flows Through the Home

❏ ❏ 52. Is the house odd-shaped: U or L-shaped (cleaver, boot), modular, etc.? Page 65

❏ ❏ 53. Is there a fireplace, stairway, skylight, or bathroom in the center of the house? Page 66

❏ ❏ 54. Are there very high ceilings, cathedral, or vaulted ceilings? Page 67

❏ ❏ 55. Are there sudden changes in the height of the ceiling in the same room or from room-to-room? Page 68

❏ ❏ 56. Are there exposed beams or roof supports? Page 68

❏ ❏ 57. Are there sloped-ceilings over sitting areas? Page 69

❏ ❏ 58. Are there very low ceilings? Page 69

❏ ❏ 59. Are there pillars or free-standing structural supports? Page 70

❏ ❏ 60. Is there a sunken living room or other rooms on different levels? Page 70

❏ ❏ 61. Are there rooms that are irregularly shaped (not square or rectangular)? Page 71

❏ ❏ 62. Is there a long narrow hallway? Page 71

❏ ❏ 63. Is there a room situated at the end of a long narrow hallway? Page 72

❏ ❏ 64. Is the house without a back door or windows, or are there rooms with no windows at all? Page 73

❏ ❏ 65. Are there rooms with excessively large windows or windows that go down to the floor? Page 73

❏ ❏ 66. Is there a close view of a tree trunk, lamp post, or utility pole through a window? Page 74

❏ ❏ 67. Does the house have all doors and no windows? Page 74

❏ ❏ 68. Does the house have a skylight or skylights? Page 75

❏ ❏ 69. Are there three doorways in a row – "a pierced heart?" Page 76

❏ ❏ 70. Are there three interior doorways very close together? Page 76

❏ ❏ 71. Are there three or more doors close together coming from different directions? Page 76

❏ ❏ 72. Does the room have double doors? Page 77

❏ ❏ 73. Are there two doorways that are misaligned – "bad bite?" Page 77

❏ ❏ 74. Are there doorways hung at an angle – "evil doors?" Page 78

❏ ❏ 75. Are there doors that open to the smallest part of a room – "contrary doors?" Page 78

❏ ❏ 76. Is there a larger doorway of a less important room opposite a smaller door of a more important room? Page 78

❏ ❏ 77. Is there an "empty doorway?" Page 79

❏ ❏ 78. Are there door knobs that clash – "arguing doors?" Page 79

❏ ❏ 79. Are there "dutch doors?" Page 80

❏ ❏ 80. Does any door open outward instead of inward? Page 80

❏ ❏ 81. Is there a spiral staircase or staircases that are steep or unsteady? Page 80

❏ ❏ 82. Are the streets to the house, hallways in an apartment complex, or the floor plan of the house like a maze? Page 81

Attracting Opportunities: Evaluating the Entrance

❏ ❏ 83. Is the view from the front door obstructed by a wall, high mountain, or high building? Page 84

❏ ❏ 84. Is there a tree, lamp post, telephone, or utility pole directly opposite the front door of the house? Page 84

❏ ❏ 85. Is the pathway to the front door obstructed? Page 85

❏ ❏ 86. Does the house lack a clearly defined pathway to the front door? Page 85

❏ ❏ 87. Is the pathway to the front door narrow at one end and wide at the other? Page 86

❏ ❏ 88. Is the pathway to the front door a long, straight line? Page 86

❏ ❏ 89. Is the front porch dilapidated? Page 86

❏ ❏ 90. Are there pillars across the front porch that give the appearance of a prison? Page 87

❏ ❏ 91. Is the front entrance recessed or hidden from view? Page 88

❏ ❏ 92. Is there an overhanging second floor balcony or excessively large lintel over the front door? Page 88

❏ ❏ 93. Does the front door have glass panels or does it look strange in anyway, e.g. like a coffin lid? Page 89

❏ ❏ 94. Is the front door too large or too small in proportion to the front façade of the house? Page 89

❏ ❏ 95. Is the garage door more prominent than the front door? Page 90

❏ ❏ 96. Does the home lack a Ming T'ang (open space) outside the front entrance of the home? Page 90

❏ ❏ 97. Does the home lack a Ming T'ang (open space) inside the front entrance of the home? Page 91

❏ ❏ 98. Is their a narrow hallway leading from the front door into the house? Page 91

❏ ❏ 99. Is there a small foyer with a wall opposite the front door? Page 91

❏ ❏ 100. Is there a split-view of the inside of the house from the front door (half wall, half open room)? Page 92

❏ ❏ 101. Is there a beam inside across the hall or foyer near the front door? Page 92

❏ ❏ 102. Is there a back door or window opposite the front door? Page 93

❏ ❏ 103. Is there a stairway from the upper floor leading directly down to the front door? Page 94

❏ ❏ 104. Are there two stairways opposite the entrance way - one leading up and one down. Page 95

❏ ❏ 105. At street level is there a stairway leading down into the main living area of the home? Page 95

❏ ❏ 106. Is the bathroom door next to or opposite the front entrance way? Page 96

❏ ❏ 107. Is there a bathroom above the front entrance way? Page 96

❏ ❏ 108. Is the kitchen next to the front door? Page 97

❏ ❏ 109. Can you see the stove from the front door? Page 97

❏ ❏ 110. In an apartment building, is the apartment entrance next to or opposite an elevator? Page 98

Rest, Rejuvenation and Romance: Evaluating the Bedroom

Before After

❏ ❏ 111. Is it difficult for the bed to be in the Command Position? Page 100

❏ ❏ 112. Is there a doorway directly in front of the bed – the Coffin Position? Page 100

❏ ❏ 113. Are there doorways on either side of the bed? Page 101

❏ ❏ 114. Is there a toilet – front or back – in direct line with the bed or any part of the bed? Page 104

❏ ❏ 115. Is the headboard on the other side of a bathroom sharing a wall with the toilet or other plumbing? Page 104

❏ ❏ 116. Is the electric box, electric devices or stove on the other side of the wall from a bed's headboard? Page 105

❏ ❏ 117. Is the bedroom an irregular shape? Page 106

❏ ❏ 118. Is there a beam over the bed? Page 106

❏ ❏ 119. Is there a sloped-ceiling over the bed? Page 107

❏ ❏ 120. Is there a window behind the bed? Page 108

❏ ❏ 121. Is there a view from the bed into the bathroom? Page 108

❏ ❏ 122. Is the master bedroom in the front half of the house or extended out in front of the house? Page 108

❏ ❏ 123. Are there bedrooms over a garage? Page 109

❏ ❏ 124. Is there inadequate space to walk on either side of the bed? Page 110

❏ ❏ 125. Does the bed position lack equality on both sides: views, lighting, space on both sides, etc? Page 110

Creating Harmony in Other Rooms of the House

❏ ❏ 126. Is the kitchen narrow and dark? Page 113

❏ ❏ 127. Can the cook be in the Command Position in order to see anyone coming in to the kitchen? Page 113

❏ ❏ 128. Is the stove opposite or adjacent to the sink, refrigerator, or dishwasher? Page 114

❏ ❏ 129. Is there a window behind the stove or is the stove next to the back or side door? Page 114

❏ ❏ 130. Is there a bathroom directly above the stove? Page 115

❏ ❏ 131. Is the dining room table positioned between two doors? Page 115

❏ ❏ 132. Is the child's bed NOT in the Command Position? Page 116

❏ ❏ 133. Is the child's room too small to position the bed against a solid wall with space on three sides? Page 116

❏ ❏ 134. Is the child's desk NOT in the Command Position? Page 116

❏ ❏ 135. Are there large windows in the children's room? Page 117

❏ ❏ 136. Is there a beam over the child's bed or desk? Page 117

❏ ❏ 137. Is there a sloped-ceiling over the child's bed or desk? Page 117

❏ ❏ 138. Is the child's room upstairs and the parent's room down stairs, or is the child's room toward the back of the house and the parent's room toward the front? Page 118

❏ ❏ 139. Does each child NOT have a space of their own? Page 118

❏ ❏ 140. Is the home office NOT large enough? Page 119

❏ ❏ 141. Is there NOT quiet or an uplifting view from the home office window? Page 119

❏ ❏ 142. Is the office desk NOT in the Command Position? Page 120

❏ ❏ 143. Is there a window behind the desk? Page 120

❏ ❏ 144. Is there a toilet – front or back – in direct line of the desk or chair? Page 121

❏ ❏ 145. Is there a bathroom door opposite the office door? Page 121

❏ ❏ 146. Is the garage NOT large enough for cars, storage, or other uses? Page 122

Wealth and Partnership Areas of the Home: The 3-Door Bagua Template

Read Page 125 to learn what the Bagua is and how the 3–Door Bagua Template can indicate a home's weak points, and how those weaknesses can be strengthened.

Before After

- ❏ ❏ 147. Is there a hill sloping down behind the house? Page 131
- ❏ ❏ 148. Are there missing corners of the Bagua, especially the Wealth or Partnership corners? Page 132
- ❏ ❏ 149. Is there an overly large extension in any of the areas of the house? Page 133
- ❏ ❏ 150. Is the bathroom in the Wealth, Health, or Partnership Areas of the house? Page 133
- ❏ ❏ 151. Are there back doors or large windows in the Wealth or Partnership Areas? Page 134
- ❏ ❏ 152. Is there a child or in-law's room in the Partnership Area of the house? Page 134

Things to Change If You Can

- ❏ ❏ 153. Are there ceiling fans over beds and sitting areas (dining table, desk, etc.)? Page 135
- ❏ ❏ 154. Are there louvered windows and vertical or mini-blinds? Page 136
- ❏ ❏ 155. Is there an electric stove or microwave oven? Page 136
- ❏ ❏ 156. Does the house have fluorescent light fixtures? Page 136
- ❏ ❏ 157. Are there interior or exterior stairs without risers – "floating stairs?" Page 137
- ❏ ❏ 158. Are there thorny or pointy-leaf plants near entrance or pathways to the house? Page 137

Things to Fix Immediately

- ❏ ❏ 159. Is the plumbing or faucets leaking? Page 140
- ❏ ❏ 160. Are their broken burners on the stove? Page 140
- ❏ ❏ 161. Are the hinges, floor boards, or stairs squeaky? Page 140
- ❏ ❏ 162. Are the windows broken or cracked? Page 140
- ❏ ❏ 163. Are the windows stuck? Page 140
- ❏ ❏ 164. Are the stairs or pathways broken? Page 140
- ❏ ❏ 165. Is the tap water undrinkable? Page 141

Change Your Location, Change Your Life
Global Feng Shui: Your Astro*Carto*Graphy Map®

Read Page 143 to learn about Astro*Carto*Graphy Maps, and if your geographical location is affecting you or your family. At the time of your birth, each planet left its unique imprint on different locations around the world. As each planet resonates with a different energetic pattern, your personality expression, emotional issues, career success, and health problems will be shaped by the planet that is closest to where you live. Even the best feng shui will be undermined by difficult "planetary" influences, while a home with what might be considered poor feng shui, will be benefited by favorable "planetary" influences. Astro*Carto*Graphy is truly "global feng shui."

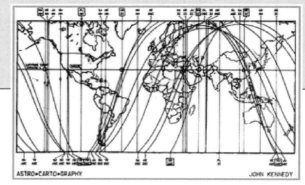

- ❏ ❏ 166. Is it difficult for you or any members of your family to live in this geographical location? Page 143

Section I
Influences of the External Environment

What Good Feng Shui Looks Like

Inside the gate there is a footpath, and the footpath must be winding. At the turning of the footpath there is an outdoor screen, and the screen must be small. Behind the screen there is a terrace, and the terrace must be level. On the banks of the terrace there are flowers, and the flowers must be fresh. Beyond the flowers is a wall, and the wall must be low. By the side of the wall, there is a pine tree and the pine tree must be old. At the foot of the pine tree there are rocks, and the rocks must be quaint.

Over the rocks there is a pavilion, and the pavilion must be simple. Behind the pavilion are bamboos, and the bamboos must be thin and sparse. At the end of the bamboos there is a house, and the house must be secluded. By the side of the house there is a road, and the road must branch off. At the point where several roads come together, there is a bridge, and the bridge must be tantalizing to cross.

At the end of the bridge there are trees, and the trees must be tall. In the shade of the trees there is grass, and the grass must be green. Above the grass plot there is a ditch, and the ditch must be slender. At the top of the ditch there is a spring, and the spring must gurgle. Above the spring there is a hill, and the hill must be deep,

Below the hill there is a hall, and the hall must be square. At the corner of the hall there is a vegetable garden, and the vegetable garden must be big. In the vegetable garden there is a stork, and the stork must dance. The stork announces that there is a guest, and the guest must not be vulgar. When the guest arrives there is wine, and the wine must not be declined. During the service of the wine, there is merriment, and the merry guest must not want to go home.

~~ Lin Yutang, 1937
quoted by James Allyn Moser
in the Integrative School of Feng Shui Class Manual

Abundance &
Great Good Fortune

House Problems With No Solutions

Houses to Avoid

The goal of life is living in agreement with nature.
~~ Zeno, 4th B.C. Greek mathematician

Below I have listed some of the most detrimental and most difficult feng shui problems to solve. These are problems that any good feng shui practitioner should check before spending a lot of time on the rest of the house. Some of these problems are modern concerns, which you will not find in books about traditional approaches to feng shui. These are problems that physically cannot be changed or easily remedied. Avoid renting, buying, or living in houses with problems like these.

If you are living in a home that falls in any of these categories, before you panic and move, evaluate if indeed you are having any of the difficulties described. Also consider how long you have been living in your home. If you have been living there for several months to a few years and you are not having problems, don't fix what isn't broken. But if you are having difficulties (though there are probably other feng shui problems), these are the ones for which there are no acceptable remedies. Again I say, consider relocating as soon as possible. The urgency of this suggestion is in proportion to the severity of health, relationship, and money problems you may already be having.

Do NOT Consider Homes With These Problems

1. Avoid extremely odd-shaped houses or houses without a clear center.

The emphasis here is on the word "extreme." There are many U, L or S-shaped houses that have acceptable remedies using landscaping and lighting. These will be described further on (page 65, #52). The overall problem with odd-shaped houses is that they have no easily defined "center" or "heart" and are therefore fragmented and dysfunctional – they are "confused" homes. Remember, whether you rent or own, a home reflects the consciousness of those living within, while those living within take on the consciousness of the house.

Extremely odd-shaped houses, even U, L or S-shaped houses, are a disturbance to the subconscious, as they lack a feeling and sense of wholeness. Whole shapes are squares, rectangles, and even circles. Qi flows smoothly through whole shapes and gets confused when the incomplete shape is getting stuck in corners or "getting lost" searching for the center.

The worst odd-shaped house I've visited was crescent-shaped – it looked like a "croissant." There was no way to bring it into balance. The physical reality of walking from one end of the house to the other has to result in imbalance, as household members career down the hallways ultimately losing equilibrium. Bizarre accidents

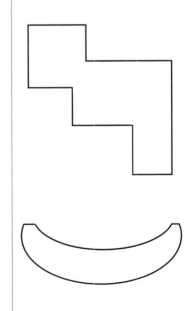

are likely. The individual who lived in the croissant-house dove into a frozen swimming pool and broke her neck. Luckily she wasn't permanently paralyzed.

Solution: There are no suitable solutions for <u>extremely</u> odd-shaped houses other than remodeling them into more symmetrical configurations.

2. Property on reclaimed wetlands or former garbage dumping site.

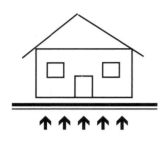

Solid ground equals stability. Beside the lack of stability, living in an area with decaying matter will eventually cause disease and ill-health, as noxious gases like radon, formaldehyde, heavy metal toxins, and so forth, continually rise to the surface.

Consider also that as the house settles, there is a great likelihood that the foundation will crack. Little cracks are often noticeable near the corners of windows and door jams of new houses built on solid ground. Consider how much more cracking will probable occur, if the house is built on land fill.

Solution: There are NO solutions for stabilizing land that is not solid or for neutralizing noxious gases rising from the substrata. The only real solution is to excavate down to hard rock before building, properly dispose of the toxic matter, fill in with quality landfill, and then this situation can be considered.

3. Property on a cemetery or ancient burial grounds.

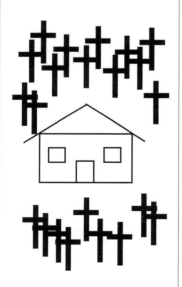

To disturb the spirit-energy of a cemetery or ancient burial grounds is to be forever disturbed by the Spirits in return. Places where the dead are or have been buried are excessively yin (soft, dark, damp, and weakening) in contrast to the best locations for homes to be built, which should be yang (light, vibrant, and strengthening).

Locations that were the scenes of violence, such as massacres, executions, or homicides should be avoided as unsettled Spirits are attracted to such places, and as these unfortunate occurrences become forever associated as happening there. This will be especially amplified if the inhabitants of a dwelling had a personal connection to horrific situations occurring at that location, as the "voices" of those who died will seem even louder.

Even without knowledge of what lies beneath the surface or how the location was once used, severe psychological problems (depression, suicidal, bipolar personality disorders) eventually can be expected among people living over a cemetery or ancient burial grounds.

Solution: At best, a ritual cleansing should be conducted by an individual of high spiritual cultivation with training in these matters. In addition to a house clearing and house blessing to remove any remaining negativity (see do-it-yourself instructions bottom page 33), a ceremony should be performed to assist any unsettled out-of-the-body entities to complete their journey to the other side. Best of all, avoid living in houses built in these kind of locations.

4. Houses built on the edge of a cliff, ravine, or gulch.

Houses built on the edge of a cliff or gulch make the inhabitants feel "edgy" and represents a life that is being lived "on the edge." This results in nervous conditions, erratic emotions, and always being anxious about finances, health, and relationships. Without a "back" to the house for support, the inhabitants will lack support and feel like they are always struggling to maintain stability in finances, health, and relationships. The subconscious anxiously awaits the inevitable land erosion that tumbles their house off the cliff and into the ravine or gulch. The closer to the edge the more unstable the psyche.

Solutions: Fences, hedges, and potted plants may provide a sense of containment for some people, while appropriate colors and images representing those areas of the Bagua affected might help overcome problems in finances and relationships (page 131, #147 – Hill sloping down behind the house weakens the Bagua Template), but it is best to avoid homes that feel unstable for any reason.

5. Houses at the bottom of a canyon wall or under a rock overhang, freeway or railroad overpass – "tiger's jaw."

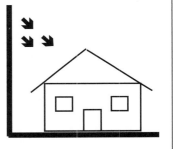

Dwellings built too close to a canyon wall or even worse, under a rock overhang, ("tiger's jaw") live in constant anxiety of being crushed by falling rocks, or literally being "devoured" by the mountain. Houses at the base of a mountainous wall in most cases do not get a full day of sun light or sun warmth, which further undermines health and can contribute to a general mood of depression, despair, and defeat. Strong winds are also likely to be funneled along the base of canyon walls, which can add to the overall disturbance of the psyche of those living too close to a canyon wall. Backache and other back problems may surface from trying to unconsciously keep the mountain's boulders from tumbling down.

This situation is even more intense under or along side of a freeway or railroad overpass, as there is additional noise and possible exhaust fumes, especially if either the freeway or railroad is exceptionally busy late at night and through the early morning hours.

Solutions: Not too many solutions to these problems. Some situations may already have sufficient trees or high hedges on either side to slow down the wind's momentum, to reduce the feeling of vulnerability and exposure. Or, it may be possible to plant trees or erect a wall. Perhaps the inhabitants are away most of the day and can get their warmth and sun light elsewhere. The anxiety of being beneath a potential "avalanche" is not likely to be mitigated by placing a mirror to deflect the negative qi or using a concave mirror facing the mountain wall to make it "smaller" and less intimidating. In short, avoid living in a house that is built at the bottom of a canyon wall, under a rock overhang , or along side or under a freeway or railroad overpass – avoid living in the "tiger's jaw."

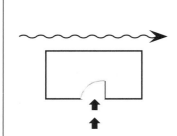

6. River, drainage ditch, or roadway directly behind or in front of the house.

River, rain water drainage ditch, or a roadway directly behind the house weakens and undermines the psychological stability of the house. Prosperity and good opportunities are metaphorically, and consequently in reality, "washed away." The faster the traffic on the roadway, or the swifter the flow of the river, the faster good fortune "goes down stream."

Likewise, a river or drainage ditch on the property directly in front of the front door can also be detrimental to any individuals living within. It is as if approaching qi is swept "down stream" or "drained away" before it even has a chance to get to the front door. It is as if someone had their legs cut off and has nothing to "stand on."

Solutions: A rarely trafficked roadway or a slow moving stream may be easier to remedy, as you can try erecting a fence or planting a hedge between your house and the fast moving road or river. However, these solutions are not likely to be very effective, if the river or roadway is loud enough to be heard throughout the day. The situation is even worse, if the noise is obvious throughout the night.

The back portion of the house should be away from busy activity. Busy activities should only be at the front of the house. Active rooms like the living room should be in the front of the house, while bedrooms and the family room should be to the back. The back of the home should be quiet, and the residents should not be disturbed by loud activities going on behind the home. Flagpoles or windsocks may work to "lift" the qi out of a shallow ditch, while being totally ineffectual in a fast moving river.

Likewise, a river or drainage ditch on the property directly in front of the front door is difficult to remedy. Perhaps a wide bridge over the river or ditch will be sufficient to reconnect the house to the world beyond. How close or far the river, drainage ditch, or roadway is to the home's front or back door may also help mitigate or exasperate the problem.

7. Excessive outside noises, obnoxious smells or toxic fumes.

We generally think of feng shui as assessing problems of structure and placement of objects in the environment. Noise, obnoxious smells and toxic fumes in the outside environment must also be taken into consideration, especially for those living in larger urban centers, where finding a home in a quiet location in a city laced with freeways and thoroughfares is often difficult.

Living near an airport of any size, along heavily trafficked streets, near loud factories or railroad tracks with trains rumbling by at regular intervals will disturb rest, distract from work, and affect intimacy, making it difficult to maintain peace of mind and family harmony.

Solutions: If you are house hunting, and you visit a house that you really consider a potential candidate for your next home, and it happens to be a week-end or holiday, be sure to go back during the week to get a true appreciation of the neighborhood

noise levels, especially during rush hour. If you work at home, neighborhood noise will be of a greater concern, so evaluate this one carefully. Also consider, that the closer you are to roadway noise, the closer you are to automotive emissions, dirt, and debris.

If you leave every morning for work and do not come home until evening, the noise level from busy, fast-moving roadways or factories may not be so overwhelming. As the roadway or factory is likely to quiet down during the evening hours, by the time you come home you should be able to enjoy your evening meal and sleep in restful quiet. In many situations, keeping windows closed and playing music that you find appealing will be sufficient to mask the outside noise. However, if it is not possible to drown out the outside noise, seriously consider living somewhere else.

Likewise, while noise might be masked, though burning incense or diffusing essential oils might mask odors coming from outside, not much can be done to mitigate the health risks of living near a city garbage dump, chemical manufacturing plant, sewage treatment plant, or other sources of foul smells and toxic pollutants all of which can be quite unhealthy. Perhaps you need to evaluate why you choose to live in a basically unhealthy environment? Consider moving as soon as possible. Remember, choosing a home is also choosing a healthy lifestyle.

8. House close to utility pole transformer, power generator stations or substations, pylon, cell phone microwave dish installations, airport radar, or nuclear power plant.

The question here is, "How close is too close?" Twenty-five yards is definitely too close. Even fifty yards is probably too close to a transformer can on a utility pole. One hundred yards or two hundred yards? What is too close to a power generator station or substation? Is a mile or two miles sufficient to avoid the harmful effects of Doppler radar emanations? Within fifty miles is probably too close to a nuclear power plant.

Take into consideration not just the actual physical reality of how close as determined by measurement, but also take into consideration the current state of your health. Do you already have various ailments specifically of the immune, hormonal, or nervous systems? Or any degenerative diseases such as cancer, fibromyalgia, heart disease, or _____ (fill in the blank)? If the answer is "yes" to health concerns similar to these, then don't even think of submitting your fragile, weak body to further insult.

Solution: If you have been living in close proximity to any of the above sources of debilitating electromagnetic, microwave or nuclear radiation, move immediately. Find the most restful home situation, get on a good detox program, and get support from an experienced healthcare professional. Filling the home with potted plants and wearing one of the various neutralizers currently being sold will do much to diminish the otherwise harmful effects of these debilitating waves. But I wouldn't count on it. The only way you would know if it works is if you don't succumb to some illness of a compromised immune system. Make the choice to live a good distance from these life diminishing situations.

Gathering Clues About a Home's Feng Shui
The Law of the Predecessors

Home is where the heart is
And my heart is anywhere you are....
~~ Lyrics by Elvis Presley

It is a very ancient feng shui belief that each home has an energetic blueprint. This energetic blueprint will affect the inhabitants of a dwelling just as a container will shape whatever substance is poured into it. The Law of the Predecessors considers that the fate of previous occupants is likely to be the fate of all occupants in the future; as all occupants will ultimately be shaped by the container they are living in and subjected to the same configurations and energetic flow of qi.

This is also evident in how the home absorbs the vibrations of previous tenants. If there was a tragic death, that energy becomes part of the energy of the structure of that dwelling. Over the years I have met many real estate agents who concur that some homes "feel" happy and some "feel" sorrowful, and that some rooms within a home may "feel" happy or sad.

It is for this reason that homes sold due to foreclosure can be assumed to be homes with unfortunate money karma. Homes sold as a result of long debilitating illness ending in a tragic or untimely death are likely to indicate homes that will adversely affect all future occupants with ill-health or early and unexpected death.

A few years ago while house hunting, my wife and I entered a home and I immediately observed feng shui indicators for difficulties in relationships. We spoke to the current tenant, who was showing the home, and discovered he was trying to find someone to take over the lease so he could move to a new dwelling. I encouragingly stated, "I hope you are moving to a finer home?" "No," he gloomily replied. "Actually, my wife and I just divorced, and I am moving to a smaller studio." Without further ado, we went to the next house on our list. Essentially, it was this experience and many others over the next months of house hunting that led to the Feng Shui Checklist approach of this book.

Space Clearing / House Blessings

Regardless of what you have discovered about the former residents, it is very important to do a house blessing and a land clearing. As you do the blessing and clearing, it is essential that you do it with the awareness that you are clearing out all predecessor–energy and as a way to establish your own presence. House blessings and space clearings can be done with three sticks of incense symbolizing the Trinity, smudging with burning

sage, ringing bells, or sprinkling sea salt around the outside periphery of the dwelling. If you live in an apartment or attached dwelling, walk around the inside periphery ringing your bells, cymbals or bowls, sprinkling sea salt, and saying your prayers. Prayerful awareness is most important when clearing negativity and attracting good fortune.

As you recite your prayers, do so with the awareness that you are "affixing" your prayer to the ever expanding smoke or sound, so your prayer "expands infinitely." As crystals refract light, the sprinkling of a few grains of sea salt around the periphery illuminates a so-called energetic dome around your home, while the sea salt anchors your awareness of this energetic dome. It is not so much for protection, as it is for establishing the parameters of your sense of personal space. You claim it, and it is yours. No other energy (i.e. thought forms) can enter your space without your permission. In this way you do not have to ward off negativity, as any negativity coming in your direction will detour, flow around your "dome," and continue on elsewhere.

Altering the Fate of a House

The Law of Predecessors states: "What has happened to previous tenants undoubtedly will happen to future occupants, if the future occupants are not aware of the ability of feng shui to alter that environment." Understandably, some situations cannot be altered. In "House Problems With No Remedies: Houses to Avoid" (page 27), there is a list of eight situations that are either impossible to change, highly unlikely to be changed, and/or are not worth the effort to change, such as, a power transformer on a utility pole within 25 yards of a bedroom, or a house built on swamp land or landfill. In these situations the Law of the Predecessor will not be altered.

The majority of the remaining situations can be considered as potentially changeable, depending on the severity of the situation. Again, some may ultimately be deemed unworkable. Consider beams for example: Is there one situated over beds, desks, and other frequently used locations? If so, how large is it? How close or high up is it? Can it be painted, rounded, or decorated to mitigate it in some way? If yes, the new inhabitants will be able to avoid the destructive effects of living under a "weight-bearing" beam. If not, future tenants can be expected to suffer the same unfortunate fate as the previous tenant who "buckled" under the downward pushing pressure of the same beam.

Same House, Different Utilization

Beside the actual configuration of the structure and its relationship to the surrounding environment, factors that can not be changed, new tenants can utilize the interior very differently than previous tenants. Factors that can be altered that might have brought misfortune to the previous tenants are: "hidden arrows" emanating from sharp-edged furniture in proximity to the bed, desk, or other areas of frequent use, or the position of a bed in direct line of the door into the bedroom, or allowing the front entrance way to become overgrown and in disrepair.

And always the question has to be asked about any feng shui solution, "Is this a band-aid or a cure?" Realistically, very few homes for sale were built with an innate sense of good feng shui. Homes that are built by people applying feng shui principles are usually homes that were built for personal use and are not likely to be for sale. Consequently, in lieu of actually building your own home, consider that any home you buy or rent will be flawed and will require a few significant feng shui corrections.

As always, first the severity of the problem needs to be determined, and then the appropriate remedies need to be put in place to transform the house into a dwelling of health, harmony, and prosperity. Almost every problem has an acceptable solution, which is why using feng shui principles and concepts to analyze a home is so important.

One way to get some clues as to what a home has in store for you is to research, if possible, the lives of those who preceded you. Then, as you continue reading the questions on the Feng Shui Checklist, look for clues in the structure of the house that may reflect eventual problems in your finances, love life, or health. But, even if the feng shui indicates there should be a problem, and no one is experiencing a problem, don't fix what isn't broken. Simply watch and pay attention to future developments.

Remember, just because your predecessors may have had problems, does not mean you will. Their problems may be due to how they utilized the space. Your advantage over those who came before you is that you have the benefits of feng shui to guide you.

**On the Feng Shui Checklist Worksheet answer
the following questions pertaining
to the previous tenants:**

9. **Were the previous owners financially successful? After this house, did they move up in life to a better situation (leave box blank)? Or down? If so ☑ the box.**

10. **Did the previous owners or tenants have serious relationship problems?**

11. **Did the previous owners or tenants have serious health problems?**

12. **Did the previous owners or tenants have other major problems to consider?**

First Criteria

Does It Meet Your Needs?

There's no place like home.
~~ Dorothy in *The Wizard of Oz*

O f course many homes for rent or sale that you will walk into will not have any appeal to you. This may be because of the neighborhood, the condition of the dwelling, or some unexplainable feeling that prompts you to recoil and exit without hesitation. Then there will be those houses that you will consider thoughtfully enough that, if indeed they are contenders, you will want to put the address on the top of one of your copies of the Feng Shui Checklist and begin an examination. Unless some feature is glaringly inauspicious, save your evaluation for when you have a quiet moment alone.

Does the House Satisfy the Basic Requirements of You & Your Family?

There are often other factors that may effect your decision, such as: availability in your price range, and or proximity to family, friends, work, school, outdoor hobbies, (beach, skiing, etc.), are all unique motivating factors to satisfy your needs or desires. Is it urban or rural? Do you prefer cosmopolitan or reclusive? Is there a home office? Is it large enough to operate a home-based business? Is it in an area of like-minded people? Does it provide the quality of life you desire? If not, remember, harboring any "complaint" will eventually find a way to express itself in your daily activities, possibly undermining your health, relationship harmony, or worldly success. It is very important to evaluate your psychological relationship with where you live.

**On the Feng Shui Checklist Worksheet answer
the following questions pertaining
to your initial feelings and needs:**

13. Does it feel good – do you like the appearance, neighborhood, views, etc.?

14. Does it offer enough space for you and your family's current needs?

15. Does it offer enough space for your needs and the needs of your family as yours and your family needs grow?

16. Does it feel safe and will it provide the opportunity for peaceful, rejuvenating sleep?

17. Is it in proximity to work and shopping?

18. If you have children, is it easy for them to get to school and to after school activities without adding stressful demands on the parents?

The Ideal House Site

Evaluating the Property

_…I have already spoken of those elevations of the ground
which indicate the presence of nature's breath, with its two currents of male and female,
positive and negative energy, symbolically called dragon and tiger.
The relative position and configuration of these two, the dragon and tiger, as
indicated by hills or mountains, is the most important point,
as regards the outlines and forms of the earth's surface._
~~ Ernest J. Eitel,
Feng-Shui: the Science of Sacred Landscape in Old China, 1st publ. 1873

The earliest applications of feng shui are examples of common sense due to one's first-hand experience of interacting with the environment. If it's cold and windy on one side of the hill, move to the side of the hill that is warm and calm. If there's no water, move closer to where the water is. And so forth.

Another important consideration in olden days was to feel safe and secure from attacking armies, thieves, and wild animals. These two basic life needs ease and safety, still hold true today and dictate the essential feng shui guidelines for all housing situations. We still consider a home's desirability by the convenience of its location and, whether we are aware of it or not, by how safe we feel.

Though marauding bandits, attacking armies, and wild beasts may not be a concern in a well-policed suburb or a gated-urban apartment complex, our concern about possible danger is still very real. The subconscious (emotional) mind, the so-called reptilian brain, still asks the question: "What if....," as it anticipates dangers like saber-toothed tigers lurking in the shadows, fears heavy objects above our heads as pending avalanches, interprets sharp points and edges as "arrows" headed our way. Even in the most civilized environments, our first priorities include finding safety and feeling secure.

19. The Armchair & the Four Celestial Animals – does the house have "backing."

Since the earliest days of feng shui practice, the ideal house site has been symbolized by an Armchair with a high back, two arm rests, and a foot stool. The high back is for comfort and support, and feeling protected from behind. Literally, the back of the Armchair reduces the tension needed to keep the spine straight, while removing the concern that if one is not careful, one can fall over, or be easily pushed, backwards. While the arm rests of the Armchair provide protection from the sides, a low foot stool in front offers additional comfort, a distant view to stimulate expansive thinking, plus an unobstructed view providing a sense of being in control. As such, the Armchair has become a metaphor in the subconscious for support, protection, and relaxation.

In ancient days this Armchair metaphor for the ideal house site was represented by the Four Celestial Animals. Just as when we were children, we looked at clouds in the sky and allowed our imagination to conjure up animal images or objects floating by, in the same way, we can now use our imagination to let the contours and natural formations of the landscape take the shape of animals and abstract forms. Allowing the imagination to roam freely over the landscape, we search for the Four Celestial Animals. In Chinese symbology, the Four Celestial Animals are the Black Turtle or Tortoise, the Azure (Blue-Green) Dragon, the White Tiger and the Red Phoenix.

The Turtle represents a mountain behind the home giving it support and protection from behind. The Turtle behind a home literally represents "financial backing." Pointed, jagged, scarred, "broken" or "sick" looking mountains or buildings generate anxiety, keeping everyone "fired" up, restless and disjointed. On the other hand, smooth, pleasant-shaped buildings or mountains behind a structure perpetuate a feeling of calm optimism, and undisturbed focus.

The high-backed Dragon and the low, broad shoulder Tiger on either side energize the site, and also offer their support. While the small Phoenix in front of the home, like a small footstool, allows for comfort and a distant view.

In a city environment this will equate to the size of buildings behind and on either side. If the terrain is flat and wide open in all directions, or one direction or the other, the support of the Turtle behind can be symbolized by a high hedge or a few taller trees. The Dragon or Tiger on either side can be symbolized by a fence or medium height hedge. Or a small house to one side and a larger one to the other.

If you are living in an apartment building, a sculpture of a turtle, or even an elephant, can be considered a "small mountain" and placed on a shelf or window sill toward the back of the apartment. Even a photograph or painting of an elephant, turtle, or of a towering mountain will give the subconscious the sense of support that it needs in order to feel safe and secure. Or at least it is worth a try.

In short, choose homes with a lush hill behind it, or if in a desert, a hill consistent with what would be expected in such an environment.

Having a home positioned on a hillside in olden days, along with a commanding view of the valley below providing a greater sense of security, has always been equated with prosperity and the ability to afford the good things life has to offer. As previously mentioned, without security there is little, if any, rest. A body unable to rest experiences constant stress and anxiety. Even the thought of an Armchair inspires rest and relaxation. This Armchair metaphor can be used in many ways, and is especially important when we evaluate the position of the bed, the desk, and even the kitchen stove.

20. The Azure Dragon and the White Tiger in proper balance.

In order to balance the fierce, yang energy of the Dragon, the subconscious needs the counter energy of the more feminine, yin Tiger with its strength and mass, taking the form of a hill or row of trees. As we project these images into the environment,

the natural balance is to let the more aggressive left eye perceive the more unpredictable, prowling Tiger, ready to pounce, on to the right of the home (as we look out). In counterbalance to the Tiger, the more joyous, yet awesomely powerful Dragon is perceived with the more intimate right eye on the left side of the house (as we look out).

The Dragon on the left side of the house is referred to as the Azure (Blue-Green) Dragon, while the Tiger on the right side is referred to as the White Tiger. Preferably, the Dragon should be higher than the Tiger. It is said that if the Azure Dragon is higher or more dominant than the White Tiger, the White Tiger is controlled by the Dragon and remains quiet. When the Tiger is peaceful, the Dragon energy is dynamized for action. If on the other hand the White Tiger is higher or more dominant than the Azure Dragon, the Tiger becomes vicious and attacks the occupants.

In natural surroundings, a hill on the Dragon-side of the house site should be higher than the hill on the Tiger-side. If the terrain is fairly or completely flat, then trees will replace the hills. If in a city environment, other homes or buildings will symbolize the Dragon and the Tiger.

This imagery repeats itself in the actual structure of the home as well. Preferably a garage should be on the Dragon-side for action, allowing the Tiger to rest. If there is a second floor to the dwelling, it too should be balanced, whereas if it is more to the left or right, it will favor either the Dragon or the Tiger. Likewise, if the front door cannot be toward the center of the structure, again the Dragon-side would be preferable.

The Dragon is male-yang energy; the Tiger is female-yin energy. In this imagery of Dragon and Tiger, we again see the necessity of balancing the yin and the yang with the Tiger symbolizing yin and the Dragon yang. A house built with a strong Tiger-side will result in a yin-yang imbalance with the woman of the house being dominant, and the man struggling to assert his identity.

Some commentators say having the Dragon-side stronger is a gender issue which favors the man of the house as dominant over the female of the house. In this way it is believed the male dominant societies maintained supremacy, while relegating woman to quieter and more subservient roles. This may indeed have been true in those societies where the man is the bread winner and must be given support for his public persona.

In our modern societies, where both men and women may have professional careers and active social lifestyles, this need for balance is still true. For these men and women, the Dragon still must be stronger to activate their public selves, and a good reputation, while allowing their feminine sides, symbolized by the Tiger, to enjoy the rest and intimacy which would be more relevant for sustaining their personal lives. Evaluate some of your former dwellings, and see how this has manifested in your life in the past and choose the balance between the Dragon and the Tiger that is right for you.

Consider which side of the house the garage, second story, and front door is on. Consider in your equation any forms in the environment, such as fences, hedges, neighboring homes or any structures that can be construed as a Dragon or a Tiger. Your final evaluation will describe the yin-yang balance of the inhabitants one to another.

"On the left dances the green dragon, On the right the white tiger is roaring; The crimson bird sings in front, At the back the black giant turtle is sitting."

~~ Ancient Text

21. Houses built on top of a hill – on the "dragon's head, back or tail."

Since the early days of feng shui, in addition to the symbolism of the Dragon on one side of the house, another is used to describe the landscape. In this metaphor we see the imagery of the Dragon's body and limbs as a way of analyzing the undulations of mountains and valleys. As part of this imagery, we consider rivers, streams, and brooks as representing the "veins and the blood of the Dragon," the wind is said to be the "breath of the Dragon," and qi itself is the very "pulse of the Dragon."

Cutting into the surface of the landscape, if not done properly, can injure the "arteries and veins of the Dragon." Such an abusive action is said to arouse the Dragon's anger with the angry Dragon bringing misfortune to those who reside in such a location. The challenge of feng shui, therefore, is to choose the most auspicious positioning for a dwelling in relationship to the Dragon's body as depicted in the illustration to the left.

It should be obvious how a house on an exposed mountain top can be equated to sitting on the "back of the Dragon., and why this would be considered a very unstable position. Here the winds are too strong and is considered an example of excessive qi. This uncontrollable energy is like unruly spirits flying all over the place. Hill top sites are locations more suited for temples and holy places, as they are closer to heaven and more inviting to Spirit energy, and visited only on special occasions.

With panoramic views that are fantastic, people are often attracted to building in such places, and some actually do well, finding a harmony uniquely suited to their particular personality. But more often than not, individuals living in such lofty, un-protected locations often suffer from nervous disorders, and more easily succumb to escapist addictions, such as alcohol or drugs, in an attempt to calm down and avoid the anxiety and stress generated in such exposed homes.

In a similar manner, living on the "Dragon's tail" is another unstable place to site a home, as the tail "twitches" suddenly and often violently. Needless to say, when some members of the family leave the home during the day and others stay home, whether on the Dragon's head or tail, the stay at home members will be the ones that become a source of distress to those who leave home during the day.

The best locations therefore are protected by the "body and limbs of the Dragon." One of the most suitable places to site a home would be on an outcropping of land extending like the "head of the Dragon" between its two limbs. Here you have a commanding view while being protected from behind and on both sides.

22. Soil quality and greenery.

Traditionally, another major criteria for selecting a home site was the quality of the soil. It was the belief that if plant life wasn't growing on a location, the life qi in the ground was deficient, and it wouldn't nourish the human occupants either. In fact, a feng shui practitioner without dirt under his or her nails was indicative of a feng shui practitioner who was not doing their job adequately. More experienced feng shui practitioners in olden times tasted the soil to determine if it was acidic, or alkaline.

After all, hundreds of years ago, and unlike in modern times, it was less likely that topsoil would be trucked in to turn a relatively harsh landscape into a verdant paradise. Or, that water would be piped in from thousands of miles and be used in maintaining orchards, residential dwellings, and resort hotels with lush landscaping.

Unhealthy or dying vegetation may be an indication of land that lacks vitality to support not just plant growth, but those who dwell in the house built on that property. Patchy or barren spots, dead trees, and scrawny weeds may indicate that life force is being drained from the house site. This needs to be carefully evaluated, as the vegetation may just be suffering from neglect, due to the lack of attention by the previous land owners. In any event, dead limbs on trees and dead or dying plants should be removed immediately. But still, questions need to be asked: Did they neglect the landscaping due to ongoing money problems? Or are the home owners already living somewhere else and figuring maintenance of the landscape will be someone else's concern once the property is sold? Is there adequate water available for landscape maintenance?

Landscape features to avoid, change, or remove if possible are trees such as the weeping willow with its droopy, weepy appearance that often reflects real sadness, pessimism, or depression. Remove "hostile" thorny plants from near the front door or along the pathway to the front door. This includes members of the cactus genus, beautiful rose bushes, or the colorful but thorny bougainvillea. I have yet to meet any home owner with bougainvillea, who has not reported being repeatedly cut and scratched by these plants in their attempt to shape or maintain them. Bougainvillea and other thorny plants are best grown on property with room to grow without need of human intervention. Unless you can find thornless varieties.

In general colorful flowers are desirable. Evergreens are preferred, as they stay green throughout the year, and therefore have come to represent longevity. Deciduous trees (trees that lose their leaves), especially in front of the home, are probably best avoided (if you have a choice), as they appear "dead" throughout the winter season, and often feel out of place in non-wintery locations like Florida, Hawai'i and other tropical and sub-tropical locales. Hedges, along with fences, are an excellent way to create barriers between the home and unsightly or aggressive neighborhood factors.

23. Rhomboid, triangular, diamond, animal, or object-shaped property.

As mentioned, square or rectangular-shaped homes and square or rectangular-shaped properties are the easiest to work with, and provide the greatest sense of balance to the subconscious.

Square and rectangular-shaped properties are often found in cities and housing developments where streets are laid out in a grid of parallel streets. Odd-shapes can be found in housing developments especially around a cul-de-sac. Odd-shape lots are also found in subdivisions, when real estate developers partition their property for maximum profit, squeezing in houses wherever they can.

Other times, how a parcel of land is divided is determined by the natural topography, when it is other natural features, such as rivers, hills and valleys, that dictate where

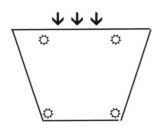

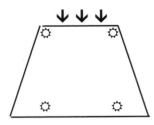

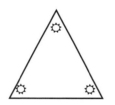

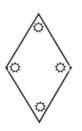

the property lines are drawn. When this occurs, geometrical shapes other than the square and rectangle usually result. Whether odd-shaped or not, avoid positioning the front door opposite an angle, and avoid having the path to the front door come from a corner of the property.

• **Rhomboid:** Rhomboid-shaped property comes in two basic types: the Dust Bin and the Money Bag. The Money Bag shape is obviously narrow at the top and wide on the bottom. The Dust bin is the opposite. Some authorities say money is easily swept into a dust bin, while others say a "dust bin" allows the money to easily fall out.

Solutions: With this in mind a "dust bin" can be modified by adding a barrier such as a hedge or fence to trap the good qi once it has flowed in, that is, bring in the sides to create more closure.

When looking into the property, if it is narrow at the front and wider at the back, this is a "money bag". This plot has no problem holding onto abundance, but may have the opposite problem of attracting the good qi to come in through the narrow opening. This can be accomplished by installing lights, landscaping, or other qi attracting features at the front of the property.

• **Triangle**: This is one of the worse shapes for a piece of property as it is difficult to site a house that will feel balanced. As with an odd-shaped house, there is a feeling of incompleteness, that something is missing.

Solutions: The larger the triangle-shaped property the more varied the possibilities of partitioning the land into usable shapes and siting the home with a sense of harmony. Hedges or fences can be used to partition while energizers like trees or lamp posts can be installed in the corners to bring some balance while strengthening the weak corners. Smaller parcels may be best avoided.

• **Diamond:** Like the triangle, a diamond-shape makes siting a house awkward. Siting a home parallel to a back or side of the property gives a sense of proportion. Furthermore, if there are other homes nearby, the corners of a diamond-shape property will be generating "hidden arrows" that shoot out at these other homes.

Solutions: Installation of lamps or flag poles in each of the corners, or appropriate hedging and landscaping will do much to bring these awkward shapes into proportion.

• **Animal shapes:** Depending on the size of the property, animal shapes can be easy to work with though positioning of the home may require some creative forethought. Understandably, avoid any property that looks like a vicious animal or one that you have a negative association with. Even if the property is shaped like an animal you like, avoid positioning the home in a less than noble part of the animal's body. Consider

if the home will be in the belly or the anus? Or, if it is being devoured by the mouth (negative), which should be avoided, or sitting at the brow (positive) and more?

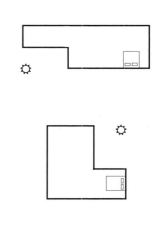

Solutions: Using landscape design elements such as planting beds, pathways, or lighting may help re configure an otherwise ugly shape and strengthen weak areas.

• **Object shapes:** Some shapes can be quite interesting and beneficial such as a Money Bag – narrow at the front and wide at the back, though two lamp posts at the narrow mouth may still be required to energize the entrance. Shapes like a Boot, Butcher's Cleaver, or Dust Pan have their own problems, and may require some creative fore-thought to determine proper positioning of enhancements to balance these difficult to balance shapes, and avoid other potential problems that come from living on these challenging-shaped properties.

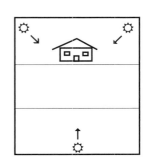

Solutions: Avoid negative objects. On properties that are shaped like a Cleaver or a Boot avoid positioning the home so it is being "booted" by the boot or "chopped" by the cleaver's blade, as depicted in the illustrations to the right. Place a mirror on the opposite wall to reflect the bed, and visually "pull" the bed back into the house.

The problem of the Dust Pan is that whatever comes in easily falls out. For a Dust Pan use hedges, trees or lamp posts to create a barrier to keep the qi that flows in from flowing easily out again.

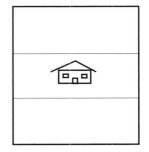

24. House situated on the front, middle or back third of the property.

Some feng shui teachers associate the positioning of the house with the success of future generations. No back yard means no descendants, or descendants that will receive no inheritance. A home with no back yard may also have difficulty getting opportunities that come "down the road", which may not be a problem, if the family is very rich to begin with. A home situated too close to a road is often equated with quick success in life, but not long lasting success, as it leaves as quickly as it came. Consequently, such a home tends to be unstable.

Solutions: Regardless of the shape or size of the property, a home sited halfway between the road and the back of the property is best. Situated on the middle third gives space between the home and the activities associated with the front of the house and its usual proximity to a road. The back of the house gives adequate space for retreat and privacy.

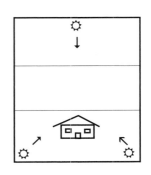

One of the best solutions to suggest for homes not in the middle third of the property is the proper use of outdoor lighting to energize and bring balance. Lamp posts should be installed on either side of the front or back of the house according to whichever side is smaller.

If you are too close to the road, try placing trees, hedges, fences, lamp posts, or water fountains to mediate. If the backyard is small, try using spotlights to lighten and

enliven the backyard qi, while "pushing" the house itself forward.

Using spotlights can be even more effective if they are mounted at the front or back corners of the property and aimed at the roof line. When the spotlights are turned on, they will "push" the house toward the center of the property. A third spotlight also aimed at the roof, should be positioned on the opposite side of the house to maintain a proper push-pull balance.

25. House built too close to the ocean or body of water.

A house built too close to the ocean will continually feel the swell of the surf with the emotional waters of the human body continually surging along with it. On calm days, emotions will be calm, and the sea will be experienced as a "sea of tranquility." But on days of tumultuous oceanic activities, lives become filled with out-of-control melodrama and crescendos of hysteria. As the subconscious never relaxes, dream-states are also likely to be disturbed and disturbing as well.

Solutions: Living near any body of clean water is considered very favorable, as water is symbolic of abundance, especially financial abundance. Facing a river, lake, pond, or ocean is especially favorable. Living too close, however, brings its own problems, such as the risk of flooding or undermining of the home's foundation. How close is too close is once again a question that requires careful consideration. It is much better to live on a hillside looking out toward the ocean which, even during high surf, appears calm, placid, and which will be creatively inspiring.

26. Mountain or large building over-poweringly close behind or on either side of the home.

You do not want a huge mountain or skyscraper towering directly behind your home. This will feel oppressive in a way that will weaken the inhabitants and lead to feelings of depression and despair. Back problems are also likely, as you attempt to "hold back" that heavy weight. Depending on the size of the mountain and how close to the house it is, this situation may be too difficult to alter. Huge buildings on either side of a house will also feel oppressive to those living in a considerably smaller dwelling.

Solutions: You can try a concave mirror to diminish the size of the over-powering building(s) or mountain(s) but this may only be a temporary solution.

27. Home located at the end of a dead-end street or a cul-de-sac.

Locating a home on the end of a dead-end street symbolizes that one's life has "no where else to go." Ideally, qi flows toward our home on roadways like a river bringing opportunity and good fortune. Our challenge is to accumulate some of this life-giving qi for our benefit and then to let it circulate away from us before it becomes stagnant, unhealthy, and unfortunate. Many dead-end streets are too narrow for the energy to circulate.

"When it comes to water, you need to observe not just the water, but you need to judge and hear the sound of water. Gently rippling, gurgling water denotes gentle and harmonious Qi flow, binging about peace of mind, a relaxed environment and good performance at work."

~~ Joey Yap,
Feng Shui for Home Buyers – Exterior

46

A cul-de-sac, like a dead-end street, also symbolizes the end of the road. However, unlike a dead-end street that comes to an abrupt stop, a cul-de-sac usually comes to an end that is wide like a full sack. The end of a cul-de-sac allows cars to make a complete turn. Also, instead of one house at the very end of the street receiving all the dead-end energy of the road that abruptly stops, there are usually a few homes situated all along the end of the cul-de-sac – all of which get "sliced" by the cars, or the road itself, as it turns in front of them.

One problem with a cul-de-sac is there is "nowhere to go" but back the way you came, so qi stagnates. Another problem is the "hidden arrows" of the cars (or the roadway itself even when there are no cars), which "cuts" into the homes lined up along the end of the "sack." For similar reasons it is better to build your house on the inside bend of a river or roadway to be embraced rather than on the outer edge where your home will be sliced (see #28 below). The outside bend of a river is always more heavily eroded as the water sweeps by. A faster moving river or road intensifies the destruction and adds to the emotional turbulence of the inhabitants' lives.

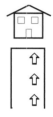

Solutions: If the dead-end street comes to a wide open field with far reaching views, or is wide enough to allow cars to make a complete turn, this may change our evaluation. One suggested cure is to mount a large mirror at the end of the road to reflect the roadway approaching it, and to create the illusion that the roadway "continues on."

"Dead-end, cul-de-sac. The names say it all. Nowhere to go."
~~ James A. Moser

If the cul-de-sac is wide enough, the residents could construct a traffic circle in the center, to allow the qi to flow in and out, while further energizing the area with a bubbling fountain in the center surrounded by flowers and pleasant foliage. With a circle in the center, the configuration is no longer a cul-de-sac, but becomes a "keyhole" instead. The wider the cul-de-sac or keyhole the better for circulating qi. In addition, each home along the curve of the cul-de-sac could mount an oval or eight-sided mirror (see Note below) over their entrance to deflect the attacking "hidden arrows," as well as put up fences and plant hedges as a protective barrier.

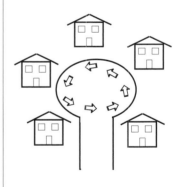

Evaluate each cul-de-sac according to how it appears and feels – wide or narrow, slightly elevated, top of a steep hill, bottom of downhill, neighboring houses jammed close together, or homes separated to allow pleasant distant views. Consider also if there is an "exit" through a backyard for security. As Grandmaster Yap Cheng Hai commented, "the problem with a cul-de-sac is that there is no exit in case of fire or danger. I have a gate in my back yard, so if there is an emergency, I can walk out into the neighboring meadow."

Keeping the qi flowing in without getting stagnant is another primary concern of those living on a cul-de-sac. If the qi comes flowing in and has no where to go, it stagnates as fresh qi has no way of getting in, consequently, those living on a cul-de-sac likewise become "stagnant" with a feeling of "going nowhere" in a relationship or a career. The challenge of the cul-de-sac is to keep the qi flowing. This can be done by hanging flags, wind socks, wind chimes, weather vanes, or banners, or sticking whirli-gigs in the lawn, or erecting a small windmill.

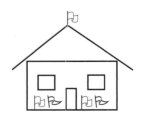

Bagua Mirror

[**Note:** A Bagua Mirror is sometimes referred to as a feng shui mirror. These are eight-sided mirrors with wooden frames usually painted red and green with eight sets of gold lines in various combinations of long lines (yang) and divided lines (yin). When a combination of three solid and or broken lines are grouped together, it is called a Trigram. As can be seen in the illustration to the left, there are eight possible arrangements. Sometimes these mirrors have yellow frames instead of red and green with one to nine dots connected by a line, instead of solid yang and divided yin lines.

These Bagua Mirrors, when hung outside the home, usually above the front door, are most specifically used to "bounce" ghosts and unsettled spirit energy away from the home, while the special arrangement of Trigrams, assigned to each of the eight sides, like a Talisman, draws auspicious energy inward. Some people will use them to bounce any negative energy away. Most important of all, Do Not hang one in your home as "negative" energy will bounce around inside, instead of away. If you do hang a Bagua Mirror on the outside of your house, try to position it so you do not bounce negative energy at the home of your neighbor. In general, any unframed, oval, or eight-sided mirror, whether concave, convex, or flat, though each having their own special application, will be as effective in deflecting negative energy that might be headed your way.]

28. Home located on outer edge of a river, roadway, or curving highway overpass?

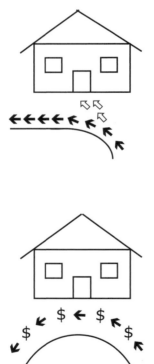

There are a few problems with any of these situations. First, there is the problem of "hidden arrows" shooting at the home, as cars come towards the house. Then there is the shape of the road itself, as if the bend of the river or roadway is like a curved sword "slicing" whatever is located along the outside curve. A variation might be two corner lots opposite each other, with one "embraced" by the cars leaving and returning, and the other, though uneffected by the cars leaving, may continually get "shot" at by those cars returning. (Compare next page, #30 – Home located at a T- or Y-intersection.)

The third problem (bottom ill. left), is that, as rivers and roads are a link to the rest of the world bringing commerce and prosperity, a fast moving river or busy trafficked street can also take money and opportunity rapidly away. The speed of loss reflective of whether the curved road is on a hill and how steep the hill is, with traffic/qi quickly coming towards the home or business establishment, and then quickly flowing away again. This is also true if your desk or cash register is situated on the outside bend of how foot traffic flows through a large office or business. Once again, money and opportunity quickly comes and, then, quickly goes.

Solutions: Ideally, a home should be "embraced" by a river/road/walk through space with qi/money/opportunity coming slowly to you, allowing you to leisurely and comfortably reach out and take what you need. This situation supports health and financial stability. In contrast, being on the outside of the river, though you see it coming, you also see it leaving.

In all of these situations the challenge is to both protect you from the "arrows",

while drawing the good qi flowing your way up to your home where it can accumulate. This can be done with hedges, driveway lights, and planting flowers along the driveways and walkways to the front entrance. Planting hedges or erecting fences can also protect the house from the "hidden arrows" shooting at the house by cars driving towards the home from either direction. But in those situations when a home is located in close proximity to the road or river, this is an inadequate solution. But even if it is, before, or until, you pack up and move, it is certainly worth a try.

29. "Tiger eyes" in the night.

"Tiger eyes" refer to the headlights of oncoming traffic, twinkling in the night like the reflective night vision of many nocturnal animals. Observing a potential dwelling by daylight may not reveal that at night time, the headlights of cars, which could be on a roadway somewhat distant from the home, are "shooting" their piercing beams into one or more of the living areas of the home. To make the situation worse, if the home is close to heavily trafficked roads, in addition to the beams of light flickering across your room(s), there will also be the continuous noise of cars clipping along the road surface.

Solutions: If there are "tiger eyes" piercing a home, try to determine if a hedge or fence can be put into place to shield you from this aggressive disturbance.

30. Business or home located at a T-intersection or Y-intersection.

Properties located at T- or Y-intersections, and in some corner lot situations (see page 48, #28 – Home on outer edge….) usually experience misfortune in health, relationship, and overall prosperity as cars driving toward the building are shooting "hidden arrows" at the inhabitants before turning away, as well as creating disturbance by braking, stopping, and accelerating again. The situation is even worse if the front door itself, or the pathway to the front door, are in direct alignment with the oncoming traffic.

Solutions: The best that can be done in this most undesirable situation is to plant hedges and erect fences. A hedge, fence or, even better, a solid wall should be several feet high. It is also a good idea to mount an eight-sided Bagua mirror to face the direction of the oncoming vehicles and will also protect the house from constantly being blasted by bright headlights, "tiger's eyes" in the night (#29 above). At least, reposition the pathway, and hope that a hedge, fence, and Bagua mirror are adequate for protecting the front door, as well as the house in general.

Deciding if these solutions are at best band-aids on a gaping wound, depends on the busyness of the street. Occasional cars headed your way will be less harmful. Constant traffic, in addition to the energy shooting at the home, also adds distracting automotive noise plus noxious gas emissions. But realize, even without vehicular traffic, the roadway itself is an "arrow" shooting at the house. Another suggested method of deflecting the "hidden arrows" of the roadway is to erect a small windmill to disperse the "killing" qi.

In Feng Shui, streets are seen as 'waterways', channeling Ch'i at a variety of speeds, from the raging rivers of interstate highways, to the meandering streams of country roads, to the stop-and-go quagmires of city intersections.

~~ Terah Kathryn Collins, *The Western Guide to Feng Shui: Creating Balance, Harmony, and Prosperity in Your Environment*

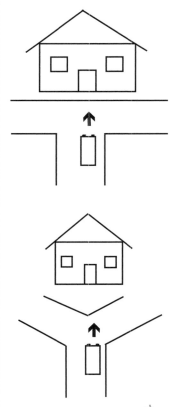

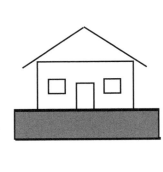

31. House on the road without a curb or step up to the front door.

The problem of a home situated at street level, without a curb or step up to the front door, is the home can easily be flooded by actual water run-off after a heavy rain, and figuratively "flooded" even when it is not raining.

Solutions: Add a curb to channel real rivulets of rain water away from the front door. In addition, this will give security to the emotional concern of "what if it does rain," even when it does not. It would also be helpful to use up-lighting, put the house numbers above the doorway, or hang a pleasant sounding wind chime or colorful windsock to "lift" the qi.

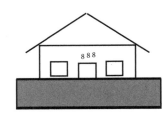

32. House or apartment situated below street level.

The problem of a home situated below street level without, a curb or step up to the front door, is an even more vulnerable situation then being at street level without a curb or step up to the front door. Not only is there worry about "what if it rains," but, "what if something drives off the street and through the window?" A general sense of anxiety also pervades due to a fear of invasion from above.

Solutions: In addition to having a curb to channel rainwater away from the home, consider a hedge or fence to provide a feeling of protection from the possibly out-of-control activity of the roadway. Out of sight, out of mind may apply in this situation. To "lift" the qi of the home, place the numbers above the door and use up-lighting. Hanging flower baskets, wind chimes, or wind socks can also be effective. Most of all, avoid further "burying" the home with hedges, fences, or hiding the entrance in any way.

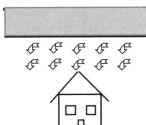

33. House down hill from a roadway.

A house below a roadway is similar to a home situated below a river or lake. Eventually, the house gets "flooded." In this case, the house gets flooded by the roadway energy along with gas fumes and noise, especially if it is a frequently traveled roadway. The situation is made worse, when combined with #34, House at the bottom of a steep driveway, which adds the "killing" energy of the cars, real or imaginary, traveling up and down. This will also be negatively experienced during heavy rains, when the rainwater pours down the driveway and floods the garage, house, or seeps beneath the foundation as an underground stream (see page 55, #43 – Geopathic stress zone under the house).

Solutions: At least make sure there are drainage ditches to properly channel the rainwater away. Position a small eight-sided mirror to deflect the "hidden arrows" produced by any cars coming down the hill toward the house. Plant tall trees or install flagpoles, weather vanes, or even spotlights on the ground aimed up to the roof line. All these devices can help "lift" the qi of a home, and thereby lift the spirits of the inhabitants promoting confidence, enthusiasm, optimism, and creative thinking.

34. House at the bottom of a steep road or driveway – an "uphill struggle."

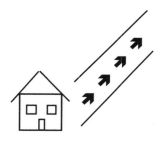

In addition to the possible flooding factor during heavy rains, there is the difficult experience of getting up the driveway. The effort needed to accelerate comes to represent effort and obstruction in other areas of life, or a constant "uphill struggle."

This is even more blatant if the car lacks power, and you have to press down hard on the accelerator in your attempt to "get up that hill." This negative influence may be increased the longer and/or the narrower the driveway actually is. The increased sense of insecurity accelerating up a long narrow driveway can certainly add to the stress of getting up that hill. On the other hand, the negative impact of "struggling uphill" will be lessened, if you remain home most of the time and do not have to make an effort to go to work each day.

Solutions: A helpful solution to counter the "life-is-an-uphill-struggle" scenario, is a lush and varied landscaping. A nicely landscaped driveway serves to pull the driver upward like tying knots in a large rope to assist the climber in getting to the top. The mind in this case is distracted by the variety and the beauty of the landscaping and is entertained on the way up lessening, and perhaps even canceling, the negative impact of the effort. A wide and nicely paved driveway enhances the effect of a pleasant drive to the top. Flagpoles, weather vanes, windmills, and spotlights can all be used with effectiveness.

35. House at the top of a steep road or driveway – "opportunities roll away."

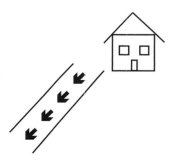

Houses at the top of a steep road or driveway experience an "uphill struggle" to get home; and even with the emergency brake and wheels turned to the curb, will feel tense and uncertain, especially when that emergency brake is pulled to its maximum. Even if you have a garage to pull into, the stress will linger.

Roadways, like rivers, are needed to bring opportunity our way. If it moves too fast, we can't hold on to it. If we sit on a hill, opportunity certainly will not flow up to us easily. In fact, when we are perched on top of a steep incline, it is easy for the good qi (money and opportunities) to flow away.

It is important to evaluate other features of a home situated at the top of a steep driveway. If there is a garage, is parking the car an easy or difficult task relative to the steep roadway? Is there at least a level lawn area between the street and the home to assist in gathering energy with foliage and lighting to catch the eye? Answer these questions carefully.

If the house and view are that wonderful, and this was the only indicator of difficulty with career and financial success, I would probably take the chance, especially if there is a level lawn. A steep lawn and difficult garage entrance, on the other hand, may sway me to avoid this house.

Solutions: Whether the hill is in front or behind a home, positioning spotlights on the downslope pointing at the roof line may be sufficient for bringing good qi back to you.

Essentially, the spotlights need to be turned on only once to establish the intention that as qi flows away, it returns to you once again.

However, once you've installed the lights, it is a good idea to turn them on from time-to-time to reaffirm this intention in the subconscious, and of course they can be used at other times to illuminate the home for special occasions and parties. Tall flag-poles along the downhill perimeter with bright-colored banners can also be used by themselves, if spotlights cannot be installed.

Another solution for keeping a home's energy from rolling back down the hill is erecting two stone or brick pillars on either side of the driveway, or some other structure, that gives the feeling of containment. Hanging wind chimes on the four corners can also do much for "lifting" the home's qi as long as they are not excessively noisy.

36. House on a one-way street.

On a one-way street qi flows fast. Houses on one-way streets are said to receive less opportunity than homes with traffic flowing in both directions. Roadways that allow for qi flow in both directions can bring opportunity from both directions.

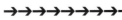

Solutions: The challenge of a one-way street is to slow the qi flow down. Narrow, meandering one-way streets, such as in small European towns, very naturally slow the qi flow down. On larger two, three, or more lane one-way streets, the speed of the road parallels the hyperactivity of those who live along the road. On a fast, wide one-way street, uncertainty, lack of stability, striving, and struggling are the norm. There's a tendency to be ever vigilant and prepared for the unexpected, and to be quick to grab an opportunity before it gets "sucked" back into the fast moving "stream" once again.

37. Parking a car pointing directly at the front door, bedroom, or other frequently used room.

As the front door is the "mouth of qi," parking a car directly in front of the front door is the equivalent of parking a car in your mouth. This blocks the home's nourishment. Additionally, when cars pull into a carport or parking area in front of a home, or even inside a garage, they shoot their "arrows" straight ahead. For this same reason of not "attacking" the entrance way, you do not want to park so your car is pointing at someone's bedroom. Even when a car is parked, and not pulling in or out, the negative effects of this "hidden arrow" will still have an adverse effect on the inhabitants.

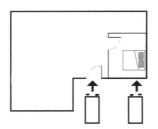

Solutions: If another parking area cannot be found, try to angle your vehicles so they do not point directly at the house itself. It's okay if the room(s) closest to the road or parking area is a utility room or bathroom serving as a buffer; or if the parking area is alongside the house, with no rooms receiving the "killing" qi. And whatever you do, do not back up into a garage if it is connected by a doorway to the main part of the house, as this forces the gas emissions under the door and into the house. This action is even worse if the door leads into a kitchen or other frequently used room.

38. High walls or foliage.

High walls or foliage, which make it impossible to see the roof of the house from the street, makes the inhabitants feel invisible. A house with high walls or foliage that cannot be seen from the street is a house that is "imprisoned."

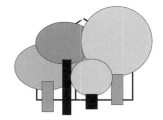

On the one hand, a high wall or foliage provides privacy, and in many cases buffers out street or even city noise. High walls or foliage can also give psychic protection to those who are insecure, afraid or who feel vulnerable being "out" in the world. But ultimately, people living in a house surrounded by high walls or foliage that totally conceal the house will feel suffocated, as positive life-giving qi cannot get in; and whatever qi is already in, will become stagnant. It is only a question of time before the residents begin to suffer from a list of debilitating problems, such as pessimism, depression, relationship stress, difficulty in healing ailments, and increasing financial woes.

The intensity of problems increases for any resident who is home most of the day. Those who leave for work, travel, or play are more likely to feel that they are coming back to a retreat, instead of being "trapped" in a prison. What is "home, sweet home" for one resident may seem isolating and alienating to another. Which means if you are the one going out each day, do not try to convince the one stuck" at home, that everything is alright, when for them, it is not.

Solutions: If the house is surrounded by an insurmountable wall, and the wall cannot easily be reduced in its height, perhaps a flag pole can be mounted on the roof or elsewhere on the property to "flag down" the qi, while reaching out into the world. If the house is surrounded by a high hedge, the solution is easy – trim the hedge. If the hedge or wall is to be lowered, it should be lowered, so that at least the eaves of the roof can be seen from the street, while continuing to be high enough to maintain privacy from the unwanted gaze of passersby and still deflect some of the street noise.

39. Frequently used rooms facing predominantly west.

The sun rising in the east is favorable for morning activities, as the sun awakens and energizes. The sun setting, however, casts a different light. The light of the sun at the end of the day has more glare. An office, kitchen, or other work space that requires focus and concentration will be most affected by this undesirable late afternoon glare.

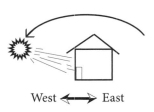

West ⟷ East

Solutions: The solution should be easy – move your work into a different room if you can, or close the curtains. It has always been a surprise to me how many homes do not have some kind of window treatment. Curtains dress up the basic structure. Ideally, they should soften a room for intimacy, as well as provide the option for closure. Curtains are needed most of all to protect the eyes from the glare of the setting sun in any activity room facing west where focus and concentration are required, such as kitchen or home office. It is an investment that will be well worth it in work comfort, minimized eye strain and resultant productivity. If you need to be in a west facing room, at least hang a lead-glass crystal sphere in the window to fill the room with rainbows.

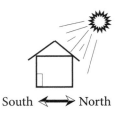

South ⟷ North

40. Frequently used rooms facing predominantly north.

From personal experience, I can assure you a house or an apartment that faces predominantly north is going to feel like a refrigerator in winter. Of course a north facing home will be a pleasantly cool dwelling during the hottest of summers. However, during fall through late spring, expect to bundle up or spend more money on heating bills.

Solutions: In addition to using central heating, space heaters, or layered clothing to keep warm, keep lights on to illuminate the space to avoid a cave-like feeling of isolation and forsakenness. A north facing dwelling is even more undesirable at latitudes that are the furthest north.

41. A pond in the backyard or to the left of the front door.

Having a pond on a property is considered very fortunate provided the pond is well kept. As long as the water is clean, a pond will bring good fortune as, once again, water symbolizes money or currency. Stocking a pond with fish generates even more currency. Obversely, a pond with dirty water represents "dirty money." Stagnant water can be a breeding ground for bacterium, mosquitoes, and algae. Stagnant water can also represent "clouded" reasoning, a sluggish body, and stagnant prosperity.

Though ponds in general are fortunate anywhere on a property, there are some locations that are considered better than others. The least favorable location is behind the house where it can weaken the support of a home referred to as the Turtle in the previous discussion of the Four Celestial Animals (page 39, #19).

Some feng shui experts say ponds should be installed only in front of the house and preferable to the left side of the entrance way as you look out. Some consider ponds positioned to the right of the home (as you look out) as an indication of eventual marital problems. A pond in the backyard can be too yin, if positioned too close to the back door of the home where it may drain finances and good health.

Solutions: Keep ponds full of fresh water. If there are to be fish in the pond, choose an odd number. Consider also choosing the right water plants such as lotus, water lily, or water hyacinth to create a low maintenance eco-system. With a little research it should be possible to have the right ecologically balanced arrangement of fish and water plants to keep from becoming a breeding place for bacterium, mosquitoes, and algae growth.

If there is a view from your window or property of a stagnant pond that cannot be cleaned and drained by you or won't be maintained by its owners, then it is necessary for you to block it from view with a hedge or fence. On the other hand, if there is any body of water within view of your home, install a mirror to reflect it into the house for increased prosperity.

Symbolic ponds, lakes, or rivers can also bring good fortune. A very large flat grassy area, whether a lawn, neighboring park, or wide-open meadow in front of the home all have the benefit of bringing financial prosperity.

42. Swimming pools.

Swimming pools are usually installed behind a home in the backyard or behind a front fence along the side of the house. Swimming pools are meant for recreation but can bring problems as well, if they are not properly placed and configured. Above ground pools should never be very close to a house, as the quantity of water will be felt as "flooding" into the home in addition to the enormous amount of yin energy it contains. This is also true for municipal water tanks on an adjacent property.

In-ground swimming pools can also have a negative effect, especially if too close to a bedroom. Problems with bladder, urinary tract, or water retention are typical. There is the additional problem if the pool is square, as the corners of the pool are considered "hidden arrows" and should not point at bedrooms, home offices, or other frequently used rooms so the people within do not feel they are being "shot" at.

Solutions: In-ground swimming pools that are kidney-shaped embracing a home are considered best. In most situations one or more potted plants can be positioned at the offensive corners of rectangular swimming pools to lighten their harmful influence. Also adding wood of any kind such as a fence, bushes, or trees near and around the pool or holding tank will help absorb the negative effects of excessive water.

A swimming pool should always be filled with water, even in winter time, to attract abundance. If it is deemed necessary to empty, put a pool cover over it, so finances will not go "down the drain."

A broken or unused pool is to be avoided. If you cannot fix it, fill it with earth before health and prosperity are "drained" away. Never allow water to become stagnant in ponds, pools, spas, cisterns, or bird baths.

43. An underground stream or geopathic stress zone running under the house – the "Claws of the Dragon."

Geopathic stress zones, also called water veins, are the result of underground moisture moving along fissures and fractures in the earth's surface. In effect, these underground streams strip the electrons as they move along beneath the earth's surface resulting in electromagnetic radiation. These radiating and often disturbing vibrations are highly charged with positive ions.

Not all underground streams are noxious and pathogenic. Some are neutral and some can be quite energizing. It has also been discovered that sometimes underground streams cross each other forming what are called Hartmann or Curry Grids. These grids are even harsher and unhealthier in their effect on homes built over them, and especially on any human trying to get a good night sleep when any of these noxious energies happen to flow under their bed. Even worse than difficulty sleeping is the likelihood of serious illnesses developing, such as various forms of cancer, multiple sclerosis, inflammatory diseases, or illnesses that seem resistant to even the best therapy, holistic or otherwise.

These geopathic stress zones can be detect by walking around the house using a

dowsing rod or holding a pendulum over the floor plan. If you do not know how to dowse, contact your local Dowsing Society and hire someone to do it for you.

Visually, pathogenetic underground streams reveal themselves in trees that lean radically or have cancerous growths on them. Mold, lichen, moss, or other growths on a side of the home or an area of the roof are other indicators, as are unusual gaps in a hedge, close proximity to bodies of water or known earthquake prone fault lines, neighbors or previous occupants who are ill, or you sleep well in another room.

Solutions: Although they can be as wide as the whole house, most underground streams are not much wider than two or three feet. Consequently, it is possible to effect someone sleeping on one side of the bed and not the other. If there is an underground stream that is disturbing sleep and undermining one's health, the simplest solution is to move the bed to a different side of the room or a different area of the house.

If the bed cannot be relocated, then it is necessary to deflect or, even better, to neutralize the stream. The traditional approach suggested by most trained dowsers is to deflect the stream using rebars pounded into the ground or blue cobalt glass. Consider, however, unless you live far from neighbors, the problem with this approach is that as you deflect the stream from your property, it is likely to effect someone living nearby.

Whether coming from underground or from the electrical appliances, breaker boxes and nearby cell phone relay towers, there are several devices now available for neutralizing electromagnetic radiation that can be worn. The products that I prefer that are least expensive and quite effective are from Biomagnetic Research, Inc. located in Globe, Arizona. As of this writing, they do not have a website. To discuss which device would be best for you, call them at: 928-425-5051.

These devices utilize a mix of ground quartz crystal, various semi-precious gemstones, several rare earth minerals and other materials to create what they call a **Crystal Catalyst®**. Apparently, this combination is fused together based on the *faience* technology of the ancient Egyptians and possibly even earlier by the Sumerians. For pathogenetic underground streams, there is the Tri-Pak Resonator (illustration to the right and also suggested on page 105, #116 – Electric box, electric devices or stove on the other side of the wall from a bed's headboard). The Tri-Pac is buried in the ground at the point the stream flows under the dwelling, just deep enough to replace the sod over it (pointed end upward/wide-side down); or a Flat Spiral Resonator that can be placed on the floor beneath the bed. I have also heard a sheet of cork works equally as well.

While you're at it, you might also want to purchase a Cell Phone Tab to neutralize those nasty cell phone microwaves, a 3-Hole Resonator to put on your cordless phone power base, especially if you are using DECT technology, a 12-Point Resonator on your monitor, if you are still using one of those old fashion cathode-ray tube monitors in your home or office, or a Clear Field Plate to protect the whole house from everything. Be sure to tell them I sent you.

"The claws of the Dragon are not just under us now, they are all around us."
~~ Charmion McKusick,
The Claws of the Dragon

Underground Stream
Neutralize with
Tri-Pak Resonator

Neighbors – Harmony In The Community

Effect Other Homes May Have on Each Other

If there is harmony in the home,
there will be order in the nation.
If there is order in the nation,
there will be peace in the world.
~~Anonymous

Roadways, roof lines, the edges of a building, the direction of pathways, driveways, and even the fencing around a neighboring property can have a detrimental influence, if they point or "shoot" directly at another dwelling. With this in mind, you do not want to live in a dwelling where roadways, pathways, driveways, and fence lines "shoot" directly at you, especially not at the front door or any of the major rooms, such as kitchen, dining room, bedrooms, or home office. The best solution in any of these situations is to hang potted plants or wind chimes. To ensure harmony between respective dwellings, plant hedges or erect fences to protect you and them from possible "hidden arrow."

One of the most obvious mistakes made in residential neighborhoods, and in commercial areas with towering office buildings, is large structures constructed among smaller ones. Take the case of the Bank of Hong Kong & Shanghai building being "attacked" by the Bank of China building. Before China reclaimed Hong Kong from the British in 1999, they built the towering Bank of China building. Not only is the Bank of China building considerably higher, and therefore more dominant than the smaller Bank of Hong Kong & Shanghai building in the lower right of the picture, but notice how the edge of the bank appears as a knife "slicing through" the British Governor's Mansion situated in the lower center. After many people working in this building got ill or had accidents, it was converted to a storage house.

Photo from Issue #22, Feb. 2000
by permission from
"Feng Shui for Modern
Living" Magazine,
(no longer in circulation).

When a new high rise, subdivision or strip mall is constructed, the qi flow of the environment changes considerably, possibly for the better, but usually for the worse. New urban developments bring urban congestion, increased air and noise pollution, and "hidden arrows" from the newly constructed wall angles and roof lines shooting in all directions. In many cases, previously built smaller one and two-story residential homes are now overshadowed and energetically "squashed" by the new larger structures which can be several stories high or even worse, a skyscraper. Hopefully, cures can be installed to block or deflect these "hidden arrows."

In densely populated cities in the Orient, almost all the homes have small mirrors mounted over their doorways. The intent of these mirrors is to deflect "hidden arrows"

that may be aiming at the front door from tall buildings a few streets away, or from "hidden arrows" being deflected off of a neighbor's mirror across the street. In Malaysia, where feng shui is very popular, I saw a photo of one skyscraper which hung a mirror to bounce back the "hidden arrows" from a parking structure across the street. The owners of the parking structure in turn installed a cannon to symbolically send the negative energy right back.

44. Neighboring roof lines, roof top antennas, fence lines, trees, and hedges.

In areas where there are many homes clustered together, it is important to observe the relationship of one house to another. You should especially observe driveways, pathways, fences, landscaping, roof lines, and the corners of structures.

The most obvious consideration is the relationship of one structure to another. In the past we have laughed at the "ticky-tacky" lineup of homes in a housing tract, boring and conducive to conformity. How wonderful it is to be a land owner, having the freedom to design and place a home in accordance to one's own individuality and desire.

Yet this freedom can unintentionally lead to community disharmony in regard to the position of the structure itself, and even choice of landscaping. It is not uncommon to see a complete disregard as to how a newly built structure may impact a neighbor's life, or even the life of the inhabitants of the newly built structure for that matter.

One problem that I often observe is the misalignment of one structure with another, whether from one property to another, or two structures on the same property. Simply stated, when the corner of one structure points at another structure, there will be discord between the occupants of those structures as the "hidden arrows" fly.

Solutions: The feng shui cure for this problem is to plant a hedge or erect a fence that is high enough to protect the house from any "arrows" pointing at it. In addition, it would be wise to hang a metal tubular wind chime to symbolize harmony between the two structures. Other gestures can be placement of fountains or garden statuary.

45. Front door consumed by a "tiger's mouth."

The "tiger's mouth" refers to a larger front entrance of another structure situated opposite a smaller front entrance way. This gives the appearance of one home being "consumed" by the opposing structure. In all likelihood, if the opposing structure has a larger entrance way than your home, the structure is also likely to be more imposing, symbolic of a high mountain to climb, or a great obstacle to surmount.

Solutions: If it is just the opposing doorway that is larger than yours, planting a hedge or erecting a fence to block your view, as you come out of your front door, should be sufficient. If the opposing edifice also towers above you, then the situation becomes more challenging, as you will internalize its presence as insurmountable, even if you aren't consumed by the "tiger's mouth." In either situation, some say to mount a concave

mirror to reflect a miniaturized image of the larger structure, thus "shrinking" its negative implications, making it less overpowering and less confrontational.

46. Neighbor's driveway & garage door opposite your front door.

When a neighbor's driveway is opposite the front door of your house, the "killing qi" of their car backing out toward your home is considered unfavorable. Even their garage door opening can feel like the jaws of a monster, or "tiger's mouth." On the other hand, if the garage door opposite your home is lined up to be opposite your garage door, equilibrium is maintained and no further action need be taken.

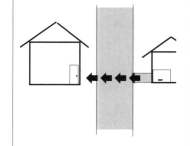

Solutions: If the garage door across the street is opposite your front door not much else can be done, but to hang a small oval or eight-sided mirror on the wall of your house opposite the garage door across the street. Remember to be careful to position the mirror so it does not deflect the negative qi at another neighbor's front door. (See Note about Bagua Mirrors, page 48 top.)

47. House uphill from another on the same property.

The problem of owning two houses with your main residence being downhill from a rental, in-law's, children's, servant's, or gardener's home is that the uphill house will tend to "lord it" over whoever lives in the house further down the hill. Those living in the uphill house, whether renter or caretaker, will act as if they own the property, and as owners, will try to control what goes on. They may even remain in their house after you, or any owner, sells the property and takes up residence elsewhere.

Solutions: To remedy this situation, the person owning the property should take their photograph, perhaps laminating it, and hang it somewhere further up toward the property line on a fence or tree, or even tack it to the back wall of the uppermost structure. Doing this in effect puts the true property owners in control by putting them symbolically higher on the hill. It is an interesting aspect of the animal kingdom to defer authority to whomever appears taller, sits taller, or is positioned higher on a hill.

48. Neighbor's house higher up the hill.

Another problem is found when one structure is higher up the hill on a different property. Again, an arrangement that is likely to result in discord, as the person living higher up the hill will try to, and probably will succeed in, "lording it" over the inhabitants of the lower structure. This will take the form of the inhabitants of the house higher on the hill complaining continuously about what the inhabitants lower on the hill are, or are not, doing to their liking.

Solutions: To encourage harmony between the lower structure and the one up the hill, consider hanging potted plants from the eaves of the roof, perhaps a sweet sounding wind chime (be sure they like the sound as well), or even installing a pleasant sounding

water fountain. However, if you do have to choose a house on a hillside street, choose a house on the side of the street with the uphill house representing the Dragon to the right (as you look at the house). If the house to the left is higher, the Tiger is strengthened and will be more difficult to bring into harmony (page 40, #20 – Azure Dragon and the White Tiger in proper balance).

49. Disagreeable or disturbing neighbors.

It is always unfortunate to live next to inconsiderately rowdy, hysterical, messy, or otherwise disagreeable people.

Solutions: Mirrors can also be used to deflect negative energy from a disagreeable neighbor. Besides freeing you of some of the impact, it actually might drive them away in their attempt to avoid having to deal with their own negative energy coming back at them.

50. Living opposite a house of worship, cemetery, hospital, mortuary, crematorium, or slaughter house.

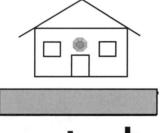

Though houses of worship can be places for joyous celebrations, they are also at times associated with suffering and death. Suffering, death, and decay are even more likely to be associated with cemeteries, hospitals, mortuaries, crematoriums, and slaughter houses. Living opposite one of these structures is especially inauspicious, as it is believed that the "spirits of the dead," pleasant or unpleasant, are attracted to such locations, and eventually will exert an undermining influence on nearby residents.

Large empty structures that remain vacant for long periods of time are considered very yin. Some individuals living next to large vacant structures may be more vulnerable to feeling a "dampening" of their own spirits as they resonate with the "emptiness" in the structure next to their own.

Solutions: Hang a Bagua Mirror (see Note page 48 top) to deflect any ghost-like energy. Say prayers that assist those of the spirit-world to know your true intent. Perhaps put guardians in the yard, such as a pair of dragon-headed Fu dogs, the mythical Chinese one-horned animal called a Qi-Lin, the fierce-looking four-legged Pi Yao, or concrete lions.

51. Living in view of a crucifix, smoke stack, or other unnatural construction.

Living in view of a crucifix on top of a church, or even in view of a tall factory smoke stack is undesirable. Like electrical lines and telephone poles, they are shapes not found in nature and are considered aggressive and attacking to the inhabitants of the dwelling.

Solutions: In this situation, unlike #8 (page 30), describing utility pole transformers, power stations, high tension wires and microwave towers that are too close to the

dwelling, here we are considering these and any other similar unnatural configuration that are close enough to be seen. As some steel towers with high tension wires, and even some utility poles look like a centipede, and as a rooster feeds on centipedes, facing a statue or figurine of a rooster in the direction of the "centipede" will destroy its negative effects.

Though it is best to avoid these images in the landscape, at least block them with trees, hedges or fences, or hang a red, green and gold Bagua Mirror to deflect any negative energy that might be coming your way (see Bagua Mirror Note, page 48).

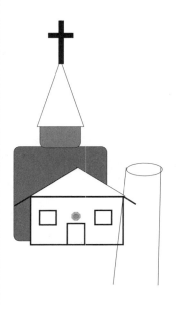

Good Luck

Section II
Interior Harmony

The Importance of Good Qi Flow

Moderation and enhancement of ch'i flow
is the underlying aim of feng shui. Good ch'i flow
in a dwelling improves the ch'i of residents.
The concept of ch'i is essential for evaluating any house,
office, or plot of land, and all their internal and external elements.
Feng shui experts act like doctors of environmental ills,
discerning ch'i circulation and pulse.
They seek to create smooth, balanced, and fluid surroundings.
For example, if three or more doors or windows are aligned in a row,
they will funnel ch'i too quickly. A strategically hung wind chime
will moderate ch'i flow. On the other hand you should look out for the oppressive,
constrained ch'i of a dark and narrow hall,
which may depress and inhibit the occupant's chances
for success in life and in work.
Proper use of lights and mirrors will symbolically
open up the space.
~~ Sarah Rossbach,
Interior Design With Feng Shui

Great Good Fortune

House Structure

How Energy Flows Through the Home

Free-flowing ch'i is like a river
stocked with the gifts of long life, prosperity, and health.
Make sure there is plentiful ch'i that flows freely through your space.
It will bring you every rich treasure you deserve.

~~ Angel Thompson,
The Feng Shui Anthology: Contemporary Earth Design, edited by Jami Lin

I t is of great importance that once the qi enters the home it can freely circulate through all of the rooms. Evaluating how the qi flows from room-to-room can be difficult to determine without training. Nevertheless, using your intuition and some of the guidelines already mentioned should assist you in making a proper evaluation. Looking first at the floor plan and then proceeding to walk through the house beginning at the front door should give you a good indication as to how the qi flows by observing where walls become blockades to navigate around, which rooms seem to pull the qi into them, which angles feel hostile, and where qi gets stagnant due to lack of circulation.

There are many minor qi adjustments that can be made to facilitate the circulation of qi. There are ways to slow it down if it is moving too fast, stir it up if it is stagnant, quiet it down if it is excessive, lift it up if it is oppressive, sort it out if it is clashing, and so forth. Then consider what you may need to do to get the qi flowing: will a mirror "bounce" it around a corner? a mobile "stir up" a lifeless corner? or will a lead-glass crystal sphere add "sparkle?" and so on. Following are some examples of how qi moves through the home and the solutions to the various problems that might arise.

52. Odd-Shape Houses - U-shape, L-shape (Cleaver, Boot), modular, etc.

A square or rectangular-shape symbolizes the earth and psychologically represents stability, dependability, and security. It is easy to control, and visually its symmetry is easy to feel in control of.

In evaluating the appearance of a house that is not square or rectangular notice what shape it is. Does it have an animal-shape? Does the animal appear to be "biting?" or is the animal friendly? If the shape is missing a corner, does it look like a "cleaver" with a bedroom on the cutting edge? Ouch! Needless to say, positioning a bedroom on the "cleaver's blade" does not bode well. If there is an important room on the "toe of the boot" or on the "cleaver's blade," place a mirror on the opposite wall to draw the bed or desk, or whatever is on the "boot" or the "blade," across the room back into the house.

To balance an L-shaped house the usual suggestion is to install a lamp post, a flag

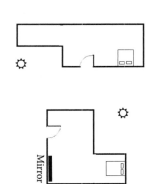

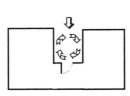

pole or plant a tree, where the missing corner of the square or rectangle would be. Filling the area in with foliage or a nicely arranged outdoor patio would also give the feeling of completeness to the shape.

A U-shaped house is not favorable as "wind" can get trapped, creating and therefore symbolizing turbulence, much as the wind on a windy day blows newspapers and other debris around and around in a doorway recessed off a city street. The best solution is to remodel that portion of the house with a solid outer wall. If remodeling is not feasible, consider a gated fence or wall that is either solid wood, brick, or stucco. A U-shape house is missing one of the sides with the corners intact. In a U-shaped house, it is easy to feel divided within or divided from the other members of the family. It could adversely affect career success if the top of the U is at the front of the house.

Needless to say, some homes are really oddly shaped and present an even greater challenge. If you can't afford to remodel, consider living somewhere else. In general, odd-shaped houses lack a "center," often referred to as the "heart," which gives a feeling of regularity and dependability. It is sometimes easy to balance a home with landscaping and placement of outdoor lights. In these situations, you need to determine what cures would be necessary to remedy the situation, how difficult they would be to implement, and, if they are worth the trouble and expense.

Modular houses with a master bedroom detached from the main area of the house tend to foster separation. Being detached from the kitchen and prime living area, inclines the relationship to also become separated. It is best to have the master bedroom and main living area, especially the kitchen, connected. Children's rooms, home offices, family rooms, and lesser important rooms do just fine when "floating" out on their own.

Solutions: A roof covered walkway would be a suitable solution for connecting the modular bedroom with the main part of the home. Perhaps adding a border of flowers or even a railing would strengthen the connection between modular structures.

53. Center of house with a fireplace, stairway, or bathroom.

In many ways, the center of the home represents the core or "heart" of the home. Whatever goes on at this location will directly affect the health of everyone who calls this structure "home."

• **Fireplace:** A fireplace has both a flue and the fire burning within. Even without a fire burning, a fireplace in the center of a house represents a "firing up" of the adrenal glands. At first this helps everyone to race around accomplishing much. But in due time, and according to age and constitution of each individual, a fireplace in the center of the house will result in the inhabitants feeling exhausted, fried, and with the adrenal glands "burned out." The chimney adds to the difficulty as it "sucks up" beneficial qi.

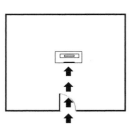

Solutions: Covering the fireplace with a curtain or screen is very important – not clear glass, but opaque. It is also suggested that three plants in ceramic or terra cotta pots be positioned in front and to the sides of the fireplace to control the over stimulating

aspect of the fire. Earthy colors or calming images may also assist in keeping the "fire" under control. The excessive Fire Element also has a way of stimulating people sitting close to a fireplace to have "heated" discussions.

Avoid putting pictures of your family and loved ones on or above the mantle of any fireplace regardless of where in the house it is located, so as not to "burn" anyone's good fortune up. Remember, the subconscious-primitive mind interprets reality differently than the so-called rational-pragmatic mind. A mirror or a picture above the fireplace depicting water or other "cooling" images would also help "cool" down the "fire."

• **Stairway:** A stairway in the center of the house, like a chimney flue, draws the energy up while also being the scene of much traffic, as individuals run up and down the stairs. This is more stressful to the heart and blood pressure than to the adrenal glands, but ultimately, it too is quite exhausting.

Solutions: A stairway situated in the center of a house needs to be anchored. This can be accomplished with potted plants at the base of the stairs and the quality of pictures that may be hung on the walls along the stairway. A 40mm lead-glass crystal sphere can be hung from the ceiling or the chandelier if there is one. The crystal sphere will diffuse the excessive qi being funneled upwards.

• **Bathroom:** A bathroom in the center of the home provides too much water and too many drains. This excess of the Water Element in the center will result in kidney and urinary tract problems, or in some it may just result in water retention.

Solutions: The excess Water Element of the bathroom can be controlled with the proper selection of colors for paint, towels, and accessories. Yellow, beige or other earth tones are colors that will absorb water. It is also helpful to keep the bathroom clean and clear of all clutter. Hanging a 30mm or 40mm lead-glass crystal sphere would also be helpful.

54. Very high ceilings, cathedral, or vaulted ceilings.

The challenge is to achieve a feeling of intimacy and connectedness, which very high ceilings and heavily sloped-ceilings tend to destroy. Evaluating a high ceiling can only be done with personal feelings. Some people like the feeling of a baronial mansion with a baronial fireplace in a baronial bedroom, and so forth. Large spaces give a feeling of grandeur and wealth. But more often high ceilings and huge rooms result in feeling engulfed by the enormity of the space and the feeling of isolation. This is even more likely in very high, cathedral, or vaulted ceilings in a bedroom.

Cathedral ceilings have the additional problem of being sloped and thereby forcing a concentration of qi to flow downward upon whomever may be sitting or sleeping on that side of the room. High ceilings at the entrance way will allow incoming qi to thin out and disperse rapidly and may indicate that along with the lack of intimacy, there is also a lack of focus and difficulty keeping things under control.

"The central area of the house is the 'central palace.' The importance in geomancy of the central palace is known in all cultures. An action at the center of a home may affect all areas, influencing the health and energies of the residents."

~~ Steven Post,
The Modern Book of Feng Shui

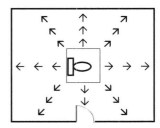

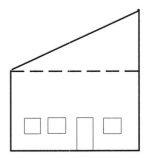

Solutions: The size of the room and the height of the ceiling may make this situation too difficult to balance. First consider existing factors like size and positioning of doorways, windows, the view out of the windows, and structural components such as beams, fireplaces, and so forth. Crown molding, wallpaper border trim, or a change in color from darker to lighter about nine to ten feet from the floor can symbolize the separation between the "heavenly" and "earthly" realms, creating intimacy below and loftiness above. Also, consider how you are going to decorate with furniture, wall art, mirrors, window treatments, and hanging plants. Remember, the goal is to achieve intimacy and connectedness.

55. Sudden changes in the height of the ceiling or low archways between rooms.

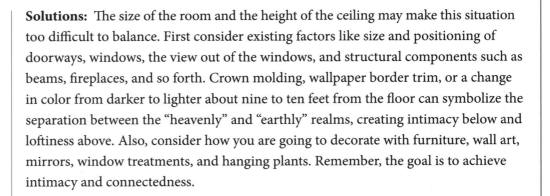

Architects can get real creative producing homes with dramatic changes in the height of the ceiling having many sudden drops from rooms with high ceilings into low passage ways or having low archways between rooms. Sudden changes in ceiling heights forces the inhabitants to "expand" and "contract" as they walk from room-to-room. The design might look good on paper, yet in reality be disastrous for those trying to live in spaces that have varying heights.

There are many varieties of drop-ceilings, from thin strips directly over the head of the bed and around the periphery of a room, to low archways dividing one room from another, to walking from a room with a high ceiling to one with a considerably lower ceiling, to someone's idea of an added-on room. Like any art project, the eye has to travel smoothly from shape-to-shape, while being aided by color, texture, and imagery.

Solutions: Many ceilings can be balanced by the judicial use of wall-hangings and up lighting provided by a torchiere lamp or wall sconce, using soft-yin elements to balance the hard-yang and the yang elements to balance the yin. Gentle moving mobiles can be hung in any corner where the qi might stagnate.

You can also fill in large wall spaces with Oriental carpets, Indian blankets, or other large decorative wall hangings or sculpture. Over low narrow passage ways you can hang decorative fans that give the illusion of an archway. Or use bamboo flutes or corbels on archways or beams to reduce the straight line and change the angles.

56. Exposed beams and roof supports.

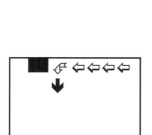

Exposed beams and roof supports, obstruct the movement of qi across the ceiling and compresses the qi, forcing it downward. Those sitting under beams or roof supports, therefore, subconsciously experience the sensation that they are holding up the beam that is holding up the roof. This will result in feeling quite stressed. Though the rational mind is quite certain the beam is firmly bolted in place, the subconscious-primitive mind continually worries, "What if it falls?"

Besides the muscular stress, depending on an individual's constitutional type, inflammation of soft tissue is also likely. In general, people will avoid sitting under a beam, and so a beam directly over a couch or armchair will often remain unused.

Solutions: In evaluating the impact of an overhead beam, take into consideration how high above the head it is, whether it is rounded or notched, and whether it is, or can be, painted the same color as the ceiling in order to diminish its intensity.

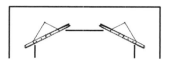

Skillfully applied *faux* finishes can create the illusion that there is no beam. In many cases, hanging fabric over exposed beams can be quite sufficient in making them disappear. Bamboo flutes or inserting corbels are also suggested as they will appear to round the arch and lift it upward. Some beams can be decorated with symbols, painted designs, or with a series of objects such as masks to help them blend in and/or allow the qi to symbolically "flow through" them. But the best beams of all are no beams at all.

57. Sloped-ceilings over sitting areas.

Sloped-ceilings over sitting areas force the qi moving along the ceiling to rapidly descend causing discomfort to those who continually sit under them. Even seeing a section of the ceiling slope elsewhere in the house can have a disorienting effect, which the subconscious mind interprets as life-out-of-balance. But worst of all is the slope coming down behind where you sleep or sit at a desk, which puts pressure and tension on the neck and shoulders.

Solutions: It is usually adequate to hang a bamboo flute with the mouth piece down and the other end pointing up at a 45° angle to reverse the negative influences of a sloped-ceiling. Larger bamboo flutes are stronger than flutes made from reeds. Bamboo flutes are often recommended as bamboo represents strength as they grow upward node-by-node. They are also resilient and have extra power as they are also musical instruments. However, not everyone can aesthetically decide to put bamboo over their Chippendale furniture, so other solutions have to be found that serve the same function. Perhaps a sculpture or wall-hanging with upward momentum? Good luck in coming up with an alternative solution.

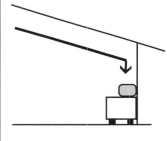

58. Very low ceilings.

Rooms with low ceilings, or rooms that are too small in relationship to the activity of the room, generate feelings of constraint and claustrophobia. A nine-foot ceiling is most comfortable, while an eight-foot, and especially a seven-foot ceiling will feel more constrictive. This is especially true for tall or large people, or in rooms filled with oversized furniture. How you evaluate this situation may depend on what the room is being used for. If the room is being used for quiet activities, it may be quite comfortable, womb-like, and intimate. If the room is designated for a busy activity, like cooking or working, such a room may make some individuals feel like they have no elbow-room and are trapped.

Solutions: Decorating with bright light, mirrors, and low furniture may provide a feeling of expansiveness in an otherwise constrictive situation. If the whole house has ceilings that feel too low, I would probably not consider renting or buying unless I

was of shorter stature, or felt I could adequately decorate to create the illusion of more spaciousness.

If you remove a low flat ceiling, exposing a peaked roof along with the rafters, be sure to cover the rafters with a new ceiling (page 68, #56 - Exposed beams and roof supports). Though giving height to the ceiling, the new ceiling will be sloped and this will make it uncomfortable to sit or sleep unless you decorate with bamboo flutes or other upward pointing wall-hangings to counter the down-pushing qi (page 69, #57 - Sloped-ceilings over sitting areas).

59. Pillars and free-standing structural supports.

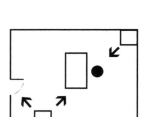

Pillars and free-standing structural supports that are rounded are better than square, as square pillars split the view and shoot "hidden arrows" in four or more directions. Pillars, whether designed as large columns or merely 4 x 4 supports, divide the view and symbolize a fracturing of one's personality. Exposed corner structural supports, though not splitting the view, are also aggressive and send "arrows" across a room.

Solutions: As with beams, it is best to remove all pillars if possible. If the pillar is structurally important, your next challenge is to decorate it by blending it into the background in order to diminish its impact. With pillars or other structural supports this can be done by training vining plants to grow around them, by wrapping them with ribbons or silk vines, or even painting flowering vines or other playful images upon them. The idea is to blend them in as part of their surroundings.

60. Sunken living rooms.

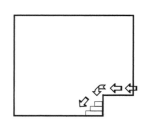

Sunken living rooms are disorienting to the psyche as the hallways and stairways of a home are like rivers and streams along which qi flows. When the qi comes to a sunken living room, it puddles and has nowhere to go, and no way to get out. It stagnates. Split levels result in split opinions, and split families with many arguments as the in-coming qi gets confused. If the energy of the home is confused, the people of the home will probably be confused too. A home with many levels can also indicate that life has many ups and downs financially and emotionally.

Solutions: Potted plants on either side of stairs leading down to the sunken living room will add some life, and help deter less observing individuals from stumbling down. As Denny Fairchild suggests in *Healing Homes: Then & Now*, "do what theatres do to avoid litigation. Outline every down stair with tiny Christmas tree lights, illuminating from the ground up. This prevents spilled drinks, hip fractures, and opens up the opportunity for a harmonious household." A throw carpet at the bottom may also provide a "landing zone," and a place to reorientate after arriving on the new level and before moving on to doing whatever you came to do. Perhaps a mobile could be hung in the most stagnant corner to keep the qi moving. Or, a 30mm or 40mm lead-glass crystal sphere in the center of the room to "lift" the qi up.

If the sunken room also has large windows or sliding glass doors, the house will "leak" prosperity like a sieve. Make sure the windows are adequately curtained and decorated to catch the life-giving qi before it flows out. In short, it is best to avoid a house with a sunken living room or lots of awkward levels.

61. Irregularly shaped rooms (not square or rectangular) or with slanted walls.

It is best when qi flows smoothly and unobstructed. Irregular-shaped rooms with many angles usually mean turbulent areas as qi gets stuck in corners "trying to decide which way to go." As someone once pointed out, "the areas of life most out of tune are reflected in the rooms most out of shape."

In rooms with many angles, "hidden arrows" shoot out accordingly. Especially important is to notice if any angles are pointing at you in your bed, dining room table, home office, or other frequently used location. I have often noticed that the area of the room on the "other side" of the angle is rarely if ever used as the subconscious avoids passing between two wall angles.

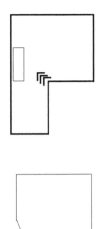

In rooms with one wall slanted inward, the subconscious need for stability is also upset and may reflect a distorted sense of reality. Or, if the room is small, a feeling of claustrophobia may result. If it is a frequently used room such as a bedroom, living room or office, a room with a slanted wall will result in anxiety, uncertainty, and poor decision making.

Solutions: In a room with many angles, the three primary ways to nullify "hidden arrows" are to remove them, block them, or deflect them. In this situation, the most obvious method is to block the offending edge either with tall potted plants, by tacking up edge-molding, or even by thumb tacking a decorative scarf over the protruding edge. Some irregularly shaped rooms are very difficult to harmonize and require great creativity in how you round that angle out or position furniture so as not to end up in a doorway or beneath a beam.

In a room with a slanted wall the best solution is positioning a mirror on the slanted-wall to reflect the opposite wall to give the impression that the slanted-wall is also properly squared off at the corners. A large potted plant in the corner forming an obtuse angle may also satisfactorily square off the room. If the room is frequently used, "squaring" is more important than if it is a room that is rarely used.

62. Long narrow hallways.

Qi moves fast in the home when it moves in a long straight line as in long hallways or from one area of the house to another without a doorway or wall to slow it down. This results in people of the house frequently racing through this area, which symbolizes "racing through life" from one location to another, or from one project to another. Always something to do, and always something to do fast. Always racing. Eventually, always exhausted. Eventually, finding it difficult to keep up. As a long narrow hallway has visual similarity to the intestines, a long hall can represent intestinal problems.

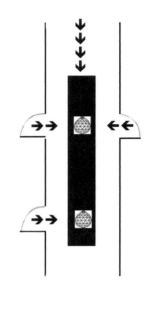

Solutions: If there are long hallways, you need to evaluate how they are to be handled, and whether the fast-moving energy they represent is also inherent in other features of the home under consideration. The longer and darker the narrow hallway is, the more foreboding and anxiety producing. So use bright colors, good lighting, mirrors, or picture art with positive images to slow the qi down.

To "slow down in life," it is essential to slow down the qi flow through the house in those places that it "races." This can be done in many ways. One is to lay down a section of carpet, interestingly enough referred to as a "runner." But it is important to choose a runner that has a meandering design on it. A design that meanders allows the eye to "meander" even if only seen with one's peripheral vision. To further assist in this meandering effect, pictures and other hanging objects can be hung on the walls to help the eye zig-zag along.

Things can also be hung from the ceiling at appropriate intervals such as lead-glass crystal spheres, wind chimes, mobiles, or whatever fits your design taste and is in harmony with the actual length of the hallway or areas of the house. Lead-glass crystal spheres are especially effective where there are doorways to rooms that are accessed along the long hallway in question. Do not put a mirror at the end of a long hallway, as that will make the hallway appear even longer. Remember to avoid creating obstructions or hanging large bulky picture frames that someone might bump into.

63. A room situated at the end of a long narrow hallway.

It is especially unfortunate to have a bedroom, office, or any frequently used room located at the end of a long hallway, as the "killing qi" continuously "bombards" those within, and especially when entering or leaving. As with a house on a T-intersection (page 49, #30), or a parking area facing a bedroom or entrance way (page 52, #37), avoid "hidden arrows" produced by fast moving qi that is moving in your direction.

A bathroom at the end of a long hallway or directly in line with the front door funnels the good qi right down the toilet. An office at the end of a long hall generates constant anxiety – like living or sitting on a railroad track. Very distracting and very nerve wracking.

Solutions: As with any long narrow hallways, the first challenge is to slow the qi flow down. This can be accomplished with a runner carpet, one long or two short ones. Preferably a carpet with a "meandering" design. If the hall is wide enough for pictures or wall-hangings, this too is suggested. At least one 30mm lead-glass crystal sphere hanging from the ceiling midway down the hall or outside the door to any room or rooms that may open into the long narrow hall will serve to diffuse the fast moving qi.

Actually remedying the room at the end of the narrow hall is more problematic. Some practitioners might suggest a mirror to "bounce" the qi away from either the bathroom, bedroom, or office that may be the recipient of the "killing" qi. If a mirror is used, it should be large enough to be able to see your head and shoulders while

walking toward it, yet small enough not to create the reflected illusion that the hall is longer than it already is. I prefer a framed-picture depicting a scene that gives a sense of depth. A framed-picture of a landscape or distant view will absorb the fast flowing qi while the glass covering the picture will bounce the qi back as a mirror would, but without the reflection that doubles the image of the hallway.

Whether a mirror or a picture, it should be affixed to the door securely. Not just hung loosely so that it will rattle and bang every time the door is opened or closed. Most home improvement stores sell tacky, putty-like stuff that can be pressed onto the back of the lower corners of the mirror or picture to keep it from moving. If a framed-picture is chosen, a non-breakable clear plastic can be used, instead of the more fragile glass that picture frames usually come with. A non-breakable clear plastic, instead of a thin piece of glass should, alleviate the "what if the glass breaks" uncertainty.

64. No back door or back window, or rooms with no windows at all.

No back door or back window is another case of the qi having nowhere to go. The qi that comes in the front door ideally circulates through each of the rooms of the house and then goes out again. If there are no back windows or doors, the qi is trapped and stagnates. Unless there is some other form of cross-ventilation, this problem of stagnant qi is more severe in rooms that are frequently used.

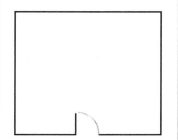

Solutions: It is important to create a symbolic back door or window using one's imagination, or perhaps framed pictures on the wall that provide the impression of looking out into the distance. It is also necessary from time to time to stir up the qi of such rooms using mobiles, aromatherapy diffusers, wind chimes, Tibetan bells, or whatever else will change the vibration and recharge it.

65. Large windows, floor-length windows, or sliding glass doors.

Large windows, floor-length windows, or sliding glass doors with wonderful views are inspirational and are especially dazzling to the visitor. However, for those living in such dwellings, picture windows, many large windows on a wall, floor length windows, or many sliding glass doors can have a negative result. Just as they allow excessive amounts of bright light to enter the room, they also allow good energy to easily leave due to lack of containment.

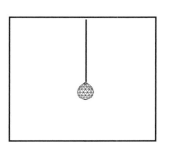

Large windows have the effect of being too distracting, undermining focus and concentration. If the view is to the west, it can also strain the eyes as late in the day, the western glare is the most intense. As one authority, Denny Fairchild, stated, large uncovered windows make a person "nervous, hyperactive, and a definite candidate for Prozac."

Solutions: In these situations it is most important to be able to "calm down" the nervous system by quieting down the excessive qi. This can be accomplished with window treatments that soften the framing of the window as it contrasts the subdued

interior with the bright exterior. Window curtains should be more than just side panels, so that when the brightness of outside is too intense, the curtains can be closed.

In addition to the window curtains, which impart a softer and more intimate feeling to the room, other window coverings can be installed to get closure or to diffuse the incoming light, such as venetian blinds, roll up bamboo, or rice paper shades. Vertical blinds and mini-blinds in most situation are to be avoided, as they emanate "hidden arrows" by slicing through the room like a "tomato cutter." If vertical, horizontal, or mini-blinds are installed, they should be kept either totally closed or completely pulled open in order to avoid their "slicing" effect (compare page 136, #154 - Remove louvered windows and vertical blinds).

For floor-length windows and sliding glass doors, potted plants can be positioned outside or inside, or a low bench or bookshelf can be used to provide a sense of barrier, especially if the windows are high off the ground and looking down creates vertigo.

To further diffuse the incoming brightness without having to close the curtains or window shades, you can hang lead-glass crystal spheres and other window decorations, such as dried flowers pressed between two pieces of glass, stained-glass window hangings, or hand-blown glass ornaments. Get creative, but don't over-decorate. Lots of smaller window panes, especially wooden window panes, reduces the negative impact of large windows.

66. View of tree trunk, lamp post, or utility pole through a window.

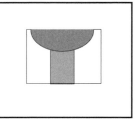

A view of a tree trunk, lamp post, or utility pole through a window affects the eyes. Just as the doors represent "mouths," the walls the "skin," and so forth, the windows of the house symbolize the "eyes." The eyes are directly connected to the liver, and in time the liver function will also be undermined by an object blocking the view through a window.

Solutions: Of course the distance from the offending tree trunk, lamp post, or utility pole is the first factor in determining the severity of this situation. It is not how far in inches, feet or yards that is of primary concern, but rather how imposing does it feel in relationship to the size of the window and the view of the obstruction. Consider whether you can decorate the section of the tree that is in view in order to soften it and make it appear more friendly and not so bold.

Decorations can include bird feeders, bird houses, wind chimes, a faceted lead-glass crystal prism in the window, or even colorful fabric strips tied around the tree trunk, lamp post or utility pole. An obstructive view from a window in a frequently used room will be more detrimental than in a room used less often.

67. All doors, no windows.

A home built without windows and all doors is an arrangement that is often found in Spanish hacienda-style houses, where double doors provide the openness to a courtyard or patio. The problem with this arrangement is that the windows represent

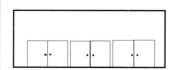

the "voice of the children," while the doors represent the "voice of the parents." They should be in proper proportion, which feng shui lore indicates to be three windows to each door.

Consequently, in a home with no windows, the children have no voice and the parents dominate. Often this results in the children having serious physical or psychological problems in their attempt to be "heard."

Solutions: Apart from relocating and finding another home to live in, pictures can be hung on the walls that appear to be window-like. Choose pictures featuring views of nature, such as landscapes, seascapes, and distant views. If possible, use picture frames with enough thickness to assist in adding to the illusion that these are the windows. The pictures need to be hung with great intention that they represent windows, or else it is merely a weak band-aid in effectiveness.

68. Skylights anywhere in the home.

In a bedroom, a skylight is like having an observing "eye in the sky" watching every action. Likewise, over a stove or desk, the excessive qi is a weakening influence. A skylight elsewhere in the home may be appropriately placed to bring light into an otherwise dark area. In an area of the home that does not receive direct light, a skylight can be thought of as invigorating. While in an already bright part of the home, a skylight can be overwhelming as excessive qi bears down upon the inhabitants and either thins out or rushes out of the house.

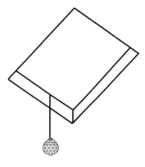

Wherever a skylight is going to be located, installing a skylight needs to be treated with great care, similar to doing surgery on the human body. Installing a skylight into the roof of a home can have dire consequences if not done with the proper respect and consideration. It is the usual lack of respect and consideration that often coincides with one of the members of the household needing an actual surgery. This phenomenon can only be attributed to the extent that people living in a home actually do become identified with their homes, and that their "home" becomes an extension of their own bodies: the doors mouths, windows eyes, walls skin, and so forth.

Solutions: To avoid this negative consequence, approach the "surgery" of the home with great respect by saying prayers, or perhaps performing a ritual that is in harmony with your religious or spiritual beliefs. To keep it simple, merely light a candle in the area of the home to be "operated" upon. Perhaps burn some incense, ring bells, and say a prayer that no one in the home will be affected by the cutting of the roof for installing the skylight, or any other major remodeling project. Give thanks and praise and see the project proceeding smoothly from beginning to end.

Once the skylight is installed, or if you rented or purchased a home with skylights already in place, it is considered good feng shui to hang a multi-faceted, leaded-glass crystal sphere from a nine-inch red ribbon. The crystal sphere will diffuse the excessive daylight qi, in addition to energizing the area of the home it is hanging in.

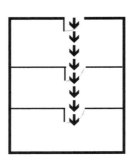

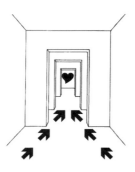

69. Three doorways in a row – "a pierced heart."

Three doorways in a row is called the "pierced heart" by some practitioners. Though the heart may not be directly affected, certainly the maladies that develop in such houses confirm there is much sadness, and that the heart is at least symbolically "pierced." It is especially detrimental to work, stand, or sit for many hours in such a situation.

Whether it is your desk, stove or dining room table, get out of the "line of fire." A desk may be easy to relocate, a dining room table between two doors will rarely if ever be used, and moving a stove is usually too costly and unlikely.

Even two doorways in a row will tend to propel us, and the qi, rapidly ahead, especially if there is a door opposite the front door. Homes with two or more doorways in a row tend to be draftier, as the qi flows quickly from one end of the home to another. This may be another reason three doorways is considered an indicator of poor health, which would be especially severe in colder climates.

Solutions: Hanging curtains on doorways or keeping them closed may be adequate, depending on how close they are to each other and their frequency of usage. A traditional approach is to hang bamboo flutes behind each door- way to draw the qi upward, while slowing it down. Evaluate this situation very carefully. In most cases, houses with three doorways in a row are probably houses that should be remodeled to remove one of the doorways. If the house cannot be remodeled, choose a different house to live in.

70. Three or more doors very close together in a row.

When confronted by a row of doors, the human response is to make a decision. Making a choice is not easy, if each door appears exactly alike. If the doors are close to each other on the same wall, the indecisiveness is increased. As in the story, *The Lady & the Tiger*, "which door is danger and which success" becomes the nagging question confronting the subconscious each time you walk towards a wall with two or more doors.

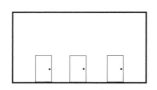

Solutions: The situation is easily rectified by hanging something symbolic on each door, giving each one a unique character or painting each doorway a different color.

71. Three or more doors close together coming from different directions.

In this situation, the problem is not so much an indecisiveness of choice – which door to choose (#70 above) – as it is an anticipation of someone, or something, suddenly emerging from one of the other rooms and crashing into you. This is often an arrangement of a bathroom between two bedrooms.

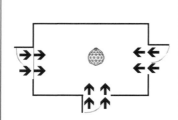

Solutions: Hanging a faceted lead-glass crystal sphere from the ceiling on a nine- inch red ribbon might be sufficient. The lead-glass crystal sphere will serve as kind of a "traffic cop" to "sort out" the qi flow from each doorway. Placing an area rug in front of the doors will also help slow the conflicting qi down by giving it a "place to rest."

72. Double doors at the front entrance or entrance into any room.

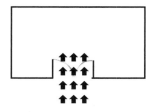

As with more than one doorway in a small area, double doors into a house or individual room, encourages a feeling of uncertainty and therefore confusion. Which door is opened and which is locked? Which is used and which is not?

Another problem caused by double doors is that qi rapidly rushes in when the doors are open or are left open. This is acceptable if the room a living room, family room, or dining room, and can be especially detrimental to health and stability if the double doors open into a bedroom or home office, and the bed or the desk is in direct line with the doorway. In these situations, disorders of the nervous system or exhausted adrenal glands can develop, as an individual in bed or sitting at the desk remains hyper alert in anticipation of someone or something unexpectedly barging in.

Solutions: One obvious suggestion is to keep one door permanently locked. If it is the front door of the house, perhaps a door knocker, or some other accessory associated with the front door can be hung on the side that is to be used, so the qi knows which door to enter through. If the double doors lead into a home office or bedroom, keep one door locked, and hang something on the door to signify which side is being used.

The aspect of the problem which is harder to remedy is the feeling of uncertainty that someone or something can suddenly barge in without warning and without the opportunity to gather one's wits, let alone a means of protection.

To help mitigate this fear and lingering anxiety, a small wind chime can be hung inside the door to draw negative energy upward or two Fu dogs (dragon headed dogs) can be place outside on either side of the entrance way as guardians. Two plants, two lions, or any imposing duo can be used to signal protection for those within. A small area rug will also assist in slowing the fast incoming qi down. All-in-all, a double door into a room is difficult to bring into balance, especially if the doors are further destabilized by being hung on an angle (page 78, #74 – Doors hung at an angle – "evil door").

73. Misaligned doorways – "a bad bite."

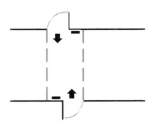

In this door arrangement, the doorways of two rooms situated off a hallway or narrow corridor are opposite each other, but are off-set, and appropriately described as "misaligned." The qi does not flow smoothly into either room. Misaligned doorways create an imbalance in the mind's constant attempt to perceive the world in balance and symmetry. One eye sees distance while the other eye is forced to focus on something nearby. If this is a frequent situation, it will result in left-brain, right-brain imbalance, emotional uncertainty, and will have an effect on physical and emotional equilibrium (page 92, #100 – Split wall as you enter).

Solutions: The remedy for this situation is to bring the two doorways into balance by hang art work to the side of one door opposite the other door, to widen the door's outline to provide a sense of depth so both eyes can focus simultaneously. How much space is on either side and the distance between the misaligned doors will determine

whether a reflective surface is needed, or if a simple wall-hanging will create the illusion that each door is actually wider and properly aligned.

74. Doorways hung at an angle – "evil doors."

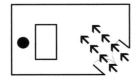

Doorways hung at an angle can be very detrimental if they open into a bedroom, as placement of the bed will be a challenge. An angled-doorway opening into a study, den, less frequently used room, or an activity room is not so problematic. Intimacy and restful security are not of importance as they would be in a bedroom.

Unless if the room is exceptionally large, most doorways set at an angle that opens into a bedroom often opens in direct alignment with the bed itself, making this a variation of the room at the end of a long narrow hallway (page 72, #63) or the Coffin Position discussed below (page 100, #112). Too much qi rushes in too fast and all at once. The unexpected can happen with no time to regain composure or to protect oneself. Preparedness for a sudden emergency needs to be maintained. Angled-doorways indicate stressful high anxiety.

Solutions: If you are stuck with a home with an angled bedroom door, close it at night. Locking it might provide a greater sense of security while sleeping. To balance the awkwardness of an angled door it is suggested to hang a 40mm lead-glass crystal sphere both on the inside and outside of the doorway. The right choice of uplifting decorative wall-hangings on walls on either side of the door both inside and outside the room will also assist in making the transition in and out of an angled bedroom door psychologically easier as well.

Unlike a bedroom, in rooms such as an office, living room, or den it is usually easier to find a location to place a desk, couch, or easy chair that is not in direct line of the angled door way. Finding the right position is also much easier if there is only one instead of a double angled door. Likewise, a single door into a child's room may not be too difficult to accommodate if the child sleeps in a single bed placed in a corner and fairly close to a wall (see page 116, #133 – Child's bed with the headboard against a solid wall with space for qi to flow around the front and on both sides).

75. Doors that open to the smallest part of a room – "contrary doors."

A door, especially the front door, should open so you can see the majority of the room. "Contrary doors" limit qi flow into a house or into a room. Not being able to see the larger portion of a room generates feelings of insecurity as the person entering does not know what to expect. If this is a frequently used door, the inhabitants are likely to feel uptight all the time with constant tension in the neck and shoulders. Frequent headaches are also probable.

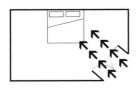
Mirror

Solutions: The best solution for a "contrary door" is to re hinge the door so it opens to reveal the larger portion of a room. If this is not possible, you can try hanging a mirror on the wall enabling anyone entering to be able to see a reflection of the larger

portion of the room, so as they enter, they feel more relaxed. This is similar to using a mirror or other reflective surfaces on your desk, wall opposite your bed, or any other situation where you cannot see the door. Note: If you use a mirror in this situation, be sure it is hung for the tallest person living or working where there is a "contrary door."

76. Less important doorway larger than the doorway of a more important room.

Whenever one door is larger than another, the larger door is perceived as intimidating to those coming out of the smaller door. This is acceptable if the smaller door is a closet, utility room, or even bathroom. It is not acceptable when the smaller door is a living room, bedroom, or home office, and the larger door is a closet, utility room, or bathroom (page 58, #45 – "tiger's mouth"). Less important rooms with large doorways perpetuate a feeling of being diminished, and eventually undermine self-esteem and sense of personal accomplishment.

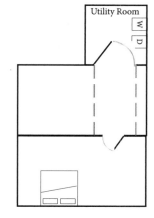

Solutions: As with misaligned doors (page 77, #73) or a split wall at the front door (page 92, #100), a mirror or other reflective surface can be mounted on the side of the smaller door to give the impression that it is larger and to give a sense of depth to enable both eyes to see deep and to maintain left-brain, right-brain balance which, when disturbed, undermines agility, and accessibility to intuitive or rational decision making.

77. An "empty doorway".

If there is a doorway that once had a door hanging in it but now is without that door, and the door frame still has cut outs for the hinges and lock, it is called an "empty door." Projects that are incomplete, household features that are broken or not working well, all affect the subconscious of the inhabitants, which will translate into incompletions and a feeling that whatever is being done is not quite complete.

Solutions: Either re hang the door or, if the door was removed for practical purposes, such as providing easy passage through a corridor or not having an open door take up wall space, then redo the door frame to remove the hinge and lock cut outs, and make the doorway into an official archway.

78. Doors that clash – "arguing door knobs."

If two doors, when opened at the same time, are positioned so close together that the door knobs will hit each other, this is called "arguing" door knobs. Consequently, this area of the house experiences constant turmoil due to the aggressiveness of the two doors banging, or potentially banging, into each other. When qi flow "clashes" anywhere in the home and for any reason, the result is that members of the household will be constantly arguing.

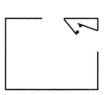

Solution: The best solution would be to re hinge one or both doors so they will open away from each other. If this is not practical, either because of financial reasons or

because the rehinged doors will be creating other difficulties, then a transcendental solution can be tried: tie a red ribbon from one door knob to the other connecting them. Leave the ends long enough to tie into bows. Once the two door knobs are connected, cut the ribbon in half and tie the ends into a bow. Now the two door knobs have symbolically become friends. A small wind chime representing harmony can also be hung from the ceiling midway above and between the two doors to bring harmony to the "arguing" door knobs.

79. Dutch doors – top half can open separately from bottom half.

Dutch doors, often associated with a country home ambience, allows one to feel "secure" by closing the bottom half, while letting fresh air flow in by leaving the top half opened. From a feng shui perspective, doors need to appear solid, so "dutch doors" are like two doors that are "incomplete" – each half being half a door.

Solution: Both halves should be bolted together and only used as a whole door. Often curtains are hung on only the upper half instead of covering both the top and bottom, giving the appearance of one solid door.

80. Any door opens outward instead of inward.

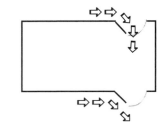

A door that opens outward "blocks" the qi flow from coming into the home. It feels awkward and aggressive having to open a door against the prevalent flow of qi. Qi flows more smoothly, and feels more accommodating and inviting, when a door opens inward. This is especially important for the front door of a residence, which needs the qi to flow in easily and unobstructed. This arrangement would also be beneficial for a place of business for the same reason.

Solutions: If the door of a home or business does open outward, obstructing easy qi flow, the door should be rehung to open inward. If it is not feasible to rehang the door to open inward, perhaps due to a municipal fire code, hanging a wind chime, 40mm lead-glass crystal sphere, and other decorations on either side of the doorway may ease the transition for the person entering to take their subconscious off of the awkwardness of having to open a door outwards in order to go inward. If a store front has an outward opening door, it may be possible during business hours, and when the weather is warm, to leave the door fully open, so customers can easily enter.

81. Spiral staircase or staircases that are steep or unsteady.

Spiral staircases are the worst architectural choices, as they "corkscrew" through the home, as if someone is drilling into one's body, and, when in the center of the home, into one's "heart." In addition to the psychological impact, they are clumsy and feel dangerous to walk up or down. Kids like to play on them and unfortunately, can easily get hurt, especially if they are metal steps with open risers.

Solutions: It is best to remove these stairs and replace with a staircase that is more secure and easier to use. If this is not possible, consider hanging wind chimes and lead-glass crystals above the staircase to protect you from their negative consequences. Placing several potted plants beneath the stair will also help to harmonize this negative feature, especially if they have open risers and "floating stairs" which are most common in spiral staircases.

If these are the only stairs connecting two levels of the home, evaluate carefully if they can be removed, or if the countermeasures suggested can be adequately applied. It is more than likely that it is best not to buy or rent a house with a spiral staircase.

82. City streets to the house, hallways in an apartment complex, or the floor plan of the house like a maze.

It is nice to be able to go straight to where you are headed. Being unimpeded in one's journey is conducive to maintaining a relaxed disposition. Hallways and stairways are conduits for qi to flow along. The qi should flow easily and unimpeded to your front door. Hallways in apartment complexes or winding street-like mazes make the qi flow confused with their twists and turns. Even though you, as a resident, may get familiar with the tortuous route, there is part of the subconscious that inevitably struggles to remember which twist and which turn to take next. The mouse eventually gets the cheese through learned behavior, as the researcher cheers it on. But the tension level remains high until the goal is achieved.

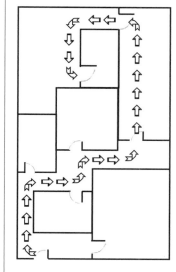

Solutions: Avoid housing situations such as these. If your circumstance does not allow for change, attempt to clearly mark your path with visual aids, such as strategically placed wall hangings or potted plant that are easy to recognize and easy to describe to a stranger, who may one day have to find the way to your home with a winning check for a million dollars.

Prosperity

Attracting Opportunities

Evaluating the Entrance

Does your front door need a fresh coat of paint? Or address numbers that shine?
Is the front lawn green or ghastly? Like a business card, your front entrance
connects the outside world with your own.
~~ Denny Fairchild, *Healing Homes: Feng Shui Here & Now*

The front door of the home is considered to be the "mouth of qi" and it is usually further designated as being the entrance way by having the home's street address near or on it, as well as the door bell or knocker. Very often the mailbox is also situated near it. It is most important that this entrance be well-lit and free of obstruction, both as you look out from it and as you enter through it.

Certainly the door itself should be of good appearance. A broken door should be fixed. A fresh coat of paint or application of a wood preservative each year is recommended to "invite the good fortune of the New Year in." Other factors should also be considered: is the front door easy to find, well-lit at night, are the pathway(s) to your door clear and unobstructed, is there a view from the door as you look out, is the space in front of your door and on the inside wide enough, and so forth.

The condition of the front door is more than just its appearance. As the "mouth" of the house, it is where the home's "nourishment" comes in. Good qi coming in equates to good health and opportunities. With this in mind, keep the front door and entrance way not only looking good, but free of obstacles and clutter so it can open wide. Notice if there are any attacking structures or forms, man made or natural, that might be "shooting" at you as you stand in the entry. If you cannot remove them, do your best to block or deflect them to ensure that only good qi comes in your front door (compare page 57, Neighbors – Harmony in the Community).

It might be beneficial to attempt to walk up to your front door, as if you are a stranger bringing those living in the house some really good news. As you approach the house from the street, be aware of how easy or difficult this task might be. Perhaps walk up with a good friend and get their feedback as well. Does your home feel abundant, welcoming, expansive, and secure? Consider all the adjustments that could be made to improve your "path in life" and your ability to attract favorable opportunities.

This exercise is especially valuable if you usually enter the house from the garage or a side or back door, and if you rarely use the front door on a regular basis. Areas of the house or apartment that are rarely used tend to be the most neglected, and yet all

"As a rule, the best entrances give an open, spacious, even grand feeling."
~~ Sarah Rossbach, *Interior Design with Feng Shui*

"The threshold, or front door, of your home is very important, as it represents your relationship with society."
~~ Terah Kathryn Collins, *The Western Guide to Feng Shui*

"When Ch'i is not accessible, you must invite it into your space and encourage it to stay. Ch'i is attracted by light, living things, and objects that catch the eye, like a beautiful painting. It is attracted to bold colors, pleasant sounds, running water, plants, and flowers. Whatever pleasantly attracts your attention, attracts Ch'i."
~~ Angel Thompson, *The Feng Shui Anthology: Contemporary Earth Design*, edited by Jami Lin

areas are internalized, and are responded to on the subconscious level. Taking a look at an area that is being neglected can be very revealing to your own process of self development. You may find the entrance way to your home is an excellent place to examine some deeply embedded core issues.

Path of Daily Qi.

If a different door other than the front door is used everyday to enter and leave the home, such as a garage door, side or back door, this door is called the "path of daily qi." This pathway in and out of the home should be pleasant to pass through, be free of clutter and obstructions, so it is easy to use, and, as with all doorways, kept clean. Nevertheless, be sure to use the front door from time to time to keep it energized.

83. A home with a view from the front entrance way.

A view from the front door unobstructed by pillars, trees, mountains or whatever is of major importance to anyone who is an innovator, an entrepreneur, or living a creative lifestyle. If the front door opens to a view, you will have inspiration and vision.

It is said that if from your front door you can only see the street, your opportunities will come only from your immediate community. If you can look out over a larger area, opportunities will come from outside your community. If you can see a lake or ocean, your opportunities can come from all over, and even from across the seas. Of course if you see a cemetery, police station, casino, or other low vibration establishment, these will define your home in a more negative way. If you aspire to be a creative artist, an innovative entrepreneur, a freelancer, or someone who lives and works independently, then an expansive view is essential to your success and recognition.

Solutions: Understandably, this may be difficult to find in large urban centers with street after street of high-rise apartment buildings. In these situations, upper level apartments with a view may be more desirable then those at lover levels. Additionally, it may be beneficial to hang pictures depicting a view near the front door as you exit.

On the other hand, if, as you step out your front door, you are visually confronted by a mountain or tall building, you may feel obstructed and overpowered. To compensate for this unfortunate circumstance, hang a concave mirror to reflect and diminish the larger structure. Installing spotlights or a flag pole behind the house may also work towards restoring some semblance of balance between your smaller structure and the one before you – like a lion with a large mane intimidating its adversary.

84. Tree trunk, lamp post, telephone, utility pole or even a fire hydrant directly opposite the front door of the house.

A tree trunk, lamp post, telephone or utility pole opposite the front door of a house is not so bad if at least 50 feet away. Closer than 50 feet becomes a serious issue depending on the size of the tree trunk, lamp post, telephone or utility pole. Even a fire hydrant in direct line of the front door can be considered negative depending if it is large

"The entranceway and everything leading up to it is a direct reflection of who you are. The entranceway acts as a transitional space that bridges your home with the environment outside."

~~ Nancy SantoPietro,
Feng Shui: Harmony by Design

enough to appear as an obstacle blocking movement (i.e. qi flow) to the front door. Any large object directly in front of the door is not only blocking beneficial qi from flowing in but is also "attacking" the health and well-being of the inhabitants.

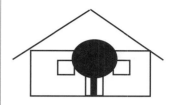

The entrance way, as the Mouth of the House, is symbolic of how the home receives nourishment. Blocking the entrance way of a home is comparable to putting your fist in your mouth, and then trying to eat. The magnitude of the difficulties to be anticipated can also be exasperated, if the tree trunk, lamp post, telephone or utility pole is at the beginning of a straight walkway leading from the sidewalk/street to the front door.

In some cases, the tree is not a straight tree trunk but rather a broad limbed, curling branched tree, such as a sycamore or old oak. In these cases, the tree trunk "meanders" and is not a "straight arrow" aimed at the door. Even so, a massive tree directly in front of the home's entrance way may still block the flow of qi. The beauty of the tree may distract from the fact that the qi flow is blocked and engender a feeling of isolation and separation from the outside world. Again, how far the tree is from the entrance way is crucial in making the decision as to whether the house you are living in or considering to buy is suitable to live in and a worthy investment.

Solutions: The most obvious first solution, in lieu of removing the tree, street sign, lamp post or utility pole that is "attacking" the front door, is to shield it with a hedge, fence or screen. The next approach would be to decorate with a bird house, bird feeder, wind chime, or strips of colorful fabric (see page 74, #66 - View of a tree trunk, lamp post, or utility pole through a window.) Installing two lamp posts on either side of your pathway may, like two sentinels, protect you from the "attacking" tree, lamp post, utility or telephone pole.

85. Attracting beneficial qi to your doorway – an unobstructed pathway.

All doorways and pathways to the house should be unobstructed as this is how opportunities come your way. But most important of all, the pathway to the front door and the front entrance way itself is the source of the greatest nourishment. It should be easy to find and easy to get to. It should have a nice meandering path to it, be easy to stand in front of, and to enter through.

Solutions: In the Orient, doorways are often painted red, as red is the color that attracts the most energy. It is highly recommended that each year, or two, perhaps at the beginning of the year, or the beginning of spring, after the severity of the winter has passed, that you apply fresh paint or wood preservative to your front door to energize its opportunity-attracting ability. Prune back foliage as needed, and replace outworn doormats with more attractive ones. Use potted plants, sculpture and whatever else might attract beneficial qi to your home.

Hanging brass wind chimes can be very beneficial, as the tubes of the wind chime funnel negative qi up and away, and the clear, crisp sound attracts opportunity to you, as you "sound" forth to the world, so the world knows where to find you. Beware,

however, that the wind chime is of the appropriate size. Bigger isn't better. A wind chime that is too big or even a small one hung in an exceptionally windy location, instead of sounding harmonious, may make a disturbingly loud clanging noise. Then, instead of attracting good fortune, will chase your good fortune away.

Placement of your street address numbers can also be used in a positive way. If they are old and corroded, trade them in for bright and shiny ones. Neither too small and obscure, nor too large and ostentatious. If possible, attach them to the siding of your house or on your mailbox, so each number is progressively higher than the last, giving an upward motion as another affirmation of your success and upward progress in life. (See illustration bottom of previous page – house numbers under right window.) Numbers angling downward or stacked with the first number on top and last number on the bottom symbolize struggle. Change the direction, and your life may change for the better. Feng shui principles can be applied to even seemingly minor details.

86. Clearly defined pathway to the front door.

No clear path to the front door equals few opportunities or opportunities that are lost. Though it usually ends in a garage, carport, or parking area, the driveway itself is also like a path. In most situations, it is adequate to have a pathway directly from the driveway to the front door. But a clearly defined pathway from the street to the front door, separate from the driveway, is best.

Driving onto a dirt lot in front of a home without a clearly defined parking area or pathway to the front door leaves too much to the imagination with the inhabitants feeling vulnerable and unprotected. This is like a covered wagon exposed on the open prairie with hostile natives attacking from all sides. Cars pulling up to the home from all possible directions constantly "shoot arrows" at the home. Landscaping and hardscaping is essential to determine from which direction the qi flows to you, and whether it feels harmonious or discordant.

Solutions: Best of all is the pathway that leads directly from the sidewalk or curb and that brings opportunities right to you. The path should be well-lit, easy to navigate, meandering slightly, and perhaps enhanced with flowering plants along its borders.

If a wide open, undifferentiated clearing is along side the house, a clearly defined driveway or pathway can be delineated with a row of painted stones, tree rounds, or even orange traffic cones. That is, something that shows people where to walk or drive.

87. Path to the front door is narrow at one end and wide at the other.

As the front entrance in effect is the Mouth of the House, if the path to the front door is narrower than the door, the occupants of the home will feel like they are "starving." This would also be the case if the pathway begins wide and narrows in width as it reaches the entrance way. If the pathway begins narrow and gets wider as it approaches the front door of the house, the occupants may feel that their "path out to the world" lacks opportunity.

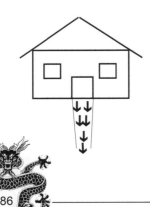

Solutions: Remedy this by making the pathway wider than the entrance way and equal in width from beginning to end. If this cannot be done, an alternative is to install two light features on either side of the narrow portion of the path; to energize that area to harmonize the flow of qi.

88. Pathway in a straight line to the front door.

Another feature to avoid is a pathway or driveway to the front door that is a long, straight line. As with all things in nature, anything that is long and straight is considered unnatural compared to flowing and meandering. Streams, rivers and pathways through the forest all meander. Anything that moves straight ahead is aggressive, like a fast moving river which erodes the soil and rips away the foliage growing along the embankment. To have a pathway or driveway go straight to the entrance way of the house is to "attack" the "mouth of the house," and its occupants will suffer. Also, like an office or bedroom at the end of a long hallway, avoid front doors that are at the end of an alleyway or pathway between two buildings.

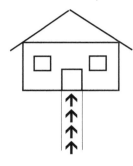

Solutions: As with all straight lines, the challenge is to transform them into flowing and meandering lines. If you cannot actually redesign your pathway with curves that meander to your front door, then try to change the appearance of the pathway. This can be achieved with various design motifs using brick work or stamped-concrete. The placement of plants, potted or in the ground, will also help. If done right, your eyes will move back and forth as you walk ahead, causing you to slow your pace, breathe calmly, and feel uplifted.

Two large potted plants on either side of the front door may also appear like sentinels guarding you from the "killing" qi coming your way. Pathway lighting is another way to alter the intensity of any "hidden arrows" from straight pathways. If the pathway is angular, it is also a good idea to use in-the-ground plantings or potted plants, bird baths, or other garden accessories to round out the edges to encourage the eye to meander.

89. Dilapidated front porch.

If the front porch is run down, in need of fresh paint, overgrown with vines, cluttered with potted plants that are not healthy, cluttered by unsightly rattan furniture, having squeaky screen door hinges or falling off its hinges, etc. etc. etc., the whole house must be a fixer-upper. Consider if you are up for the task.

Solutions: Like everything else about your entrance way: you need a clear, unobstructed path, a nice looking solid door, easy to read house numbers and so forth. The porch area should never look shabby or unkempt. Keep it clean and freshen it up with new paint when needed. If there are plants on your porch in front of your entrance way, keep them well watered, lush looking and free of brown leaves or dead flowers.

Avoid pointy-leaf plants like most dracaenas and all prickly cactus plants which "shoot arrows" in all directions, and remove spider plants which symbolize "multiplying"

problems as the new sprouts dangle, looking for a place to establish themselves and never do. All hanging baskets should be trimmed, so they do not appear droopy, which like a weeping willow, indicates sadness and possibly depression. Maintain the landscaping along the pathway and around the entrance, and great good fortune will continue to enter your life.

90. Pillars across the front porch that give the appearance of a prison.

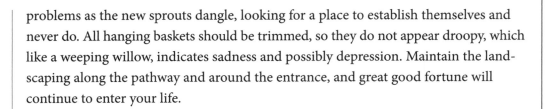

Public structures, like government buildings, are made more imposing by the careful positioning of columns and pillars. Even stately southern mansions take on a regal air. Caution, however, needs to be maintained when designing a smaller home with pillars and columns as they may result in the home being suffocated and made to look foreboding.

Though a pillar, porch column, or entrance way overhang supported by a pillar or column may have curb appeal, the main consideration is how does it feel as you exit your front door. Are the pillars too large or too close to the door way? As you exit your home, do you feel caged in? Can you see straight ahead or is your view obstructed? In a similar manner, will opportunities coming to you be blocked or diverted?

Solutions: If you have porch columns or actual pillars that are oversized or placed too close together, hanging planters or potted plants, vines or other creative solutions like wrapping the pillars or columns with colorful material may break up the cold, unfeeling, straight and perpendicular lines, and transform it into a more natural and intimate setting.

91. Front entrance recessed or hidden from view.

When we begin any journey, we feel more secure and comfortable when we have knowledge of our destination. When we begin any project, it is encouraging to have a sense of its expected outcome. Similarly, when we walk the path to our front door and cannot see the front door, we feel uncertainty. Or is a recessed front door an attempt to hide from the busyness of the world? The more difficult it is to find the front door, the more your opportunities will have difficulty finding you. This situation is made all the more difficult if, as you step out your front door, you are confronted by a fence or wall.

Solutions: This should be easy to overcome by the positioning of "guide posts" along the way with objects like a bird bath or plantings that are like friends leading us, or any one coming to visit us, down the path guiding us to the front door.

Even from the street, there should be no confusion or hesitation, as to where your front door is. Foliage on either side of the front door can give a sense of privacy but the plants should not be overpowering, scratchy (bougainvillea) or in any way obscure the entrance, as seen from down the pathway. Additional enhancements might be how you position the address of the house, a mailbox or a lawn fountain – all of which draw the eye, and the beneficial qi, forward. Hanging a wind chime to "sound forth"

and keeping a porch light on to energize the entrance way may also be helpful.

92. Overhanging balcony or an excessively large lintel over the front door.

An overhanging second floor balcony over the front door or an excessively large lintel may appear somewhat like a guillotine ready to drop. The appearance of heaviness will translate into blocked opportunities, heaviness of the heart, and ultimately loneliness and despair. (Compare page 68, #56 - Exposed beams and roof supports.)

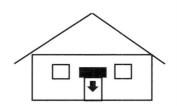

Solutions: To avoid the negative effects of an oppressive weight hanging over the front door, decorate to alter the appearance to make it "lighter." This can be done by painting the lintel, the ceiling, and the walls the same light color, as dark against light or light against dark will accentuate the heaviness of the overhang. All in all, not a good design element.

93. Doorways with glass panels or doorways that look strange.

Doorways come in many designs – plain and unadorned to richly elaborate. Some look proud, some artsy, some humorous, and some exceedingly strange, as if left over from a gothic horror movie. Like all shapes and configurations, what does the door say about who lives behind it?

Solutions: Solid wood is best. All glass is the worst – glass is easily broken and, though elegant, can leave the inhabitants feeling vulnerable and exposed. If the decision is to use a door with glass panels in order to bring light into a dark foyer or hallway, limit the glass to the upper 1/3 of the door and choose a door that appears strong and sturdy, not frail and fragile. And change the clear glass to opaque. Some doors have design motifs which can suit your tastes while others make you feel uncomfortable. It is not smart to compromise. If the door is strange, don't hesitate to change the door and get one you like and that you feel represents your energy and style.

94. Front door too large or too small in proportion to the front façade of the house.

If the doorway is too small in relationship to the front façade of the house, identities will feel diminished, resulting in conflicts and discord, as individuals try to prove themselves. If the doorway is too large, your good fortune will leak out, and there will be unrealistic goals and expenditures.

If a doorway is too small, or if it is too high and too narrow, or too low and too wide, our energetic field, often called the aura, will need to contract in order to pass through. This upset to one's electromagnetic field can be compared to being "punched" each time you walk through the door. Such a doorway is uninviting. This continual assault is experienced as emotional upset and eventually will lead to health problems as well.

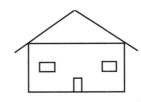

Solutions: The doorway should feel comfortable to walk through, so we feel neither cramped nor diminished. A proper proportion is at least 12" above and on either side

of us, and should be constructed for the tallest and broadest member of the family. The primary entrance way to a home should also appear to be in proportion to the design of the home's façade. The front door should be the largest door of the home. When internal doors are larger than the front door, the entrance way will be "consumed" by the larger internal door (page 58, #45, – "Tiger's mouth"). Painting the door and door frame a bright color may give it a larger appearance, while darker paint may make a door appear smaller.

95. Garage more prominent than the front door.

In older country homes, the garage is off to the side and detached from the main house, while in many subdivisions where homes are built close to the street, with narrow walkways separating one home from the other, garages are up front and prominent. With two or even three car garages stretching across more than half of the front façade of the home, cars rule. The feng shui challenge is to restore the balance, so cars serve, and we do not feel "driven." This is even more difficult when the front door is recessed.

Solutions: Avoid placing additional emphasis on the garage by decorating it or painting it with bright or sharply contrasting colors. Use muted colors or the same color as the rest of the house. Add landscaping or fences to diminish its appearance by drawing the eye elsewhere. If the only path to your front door is from the driveway, add another pathway across your lawn using decorative stone or brickwork. A row of low voltage or solar lights can also be used for accenting. Line the path with flowering plants to make it clear where the main door is, and that it is the door of greater importance.

96. The Ming T'ang – the "bright hall" in front of a home.

The Chinese expression Ming T'ang is loosely translated as the "bright hall," and refers to the openness and sense of uplift that is felt in open spaces in comparison to dark and contracted areas. In regards to your dwelling, this effect of openness is achieved if there is an open space directly in front of the main entrance, so that as you open the door you can look outward. The presence of a view translates as having "vision" for creative expression in all areas of life, just as a blocked entrance way, a recessed entrance way, or one without any Ming T'ang comes to represent feelings of obstruction in work endeavors, uninspired opportunities, and a sense of going nowhere that will further undermine health and harmony in relationships.

Solutions: Creating a Ming T'ang in a narrow alleyway or side street, or where the door opens up facing the side of another building or a fence between dwellings can be quite difficult. A large, colorful "Welcome" mat in front of the door, any landscaping or potted plants will certainly help. If it is possible, hang a picture, or paint a mural on a fence or wall opposite the front door that depicts a scenic panorama. Perhaps the scene can be a landscape or seascape showing a distant horizon. But the best homes to choose have their front doors looking out over a patch of greenery or body of water.

97. A Ming T'ang inside the front door of a home.

As you walk into the home, a Ming T'ang at the entry gives a feeling of spaciousness and accomplishment that further inspires a joy of life. It gives a place to center oneself before choosing which direction to go. It's a place to "land." There can also be a closet to hang your coat, a shelf or side table to put your keys on, and a mirror to the side to enhance the openness and allow you to see how your appearance might be. If the Ming T'ang is a small foyer, do not clutter it.

Solutions: You can try to make it appear wider and more spacious by hanging a mirror, or framed-picture with glass over the picture to give a sense of expansiveness and depth. It is nice to enhance this sense of centering with an appropriate area rug or marble-tiled area. A potted plant or a table top water fountain may enliven the Ming T'ang, while a lead-glass crystal sphere hanging on a nine-inch red ribbon might add some sparkle. Avoid putting clutter or your monthly bills on a side table with a mirror above it. Remember, mirrors double whatever is in front of them, and you do not want to double your clutter or the money you owe.

98. Narrow hallway leading from the front door into the house.

A narrow hallway leading from the front door into the house, that is only wide enough for one person to walk along, symbolizes unhappiness in relationships and a person who lives or feels alone. Unless there are some other more supportive factors, this house will not allow two people to walk and live together without contention and constant argument.

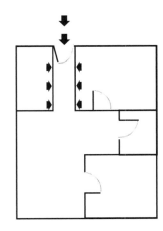

Solutions: This configuration needs remodeling. It may be possible to widen the hallway using mirrors, as long as hanging mirrors or pictures on the wall won't be bumped against, making these remedies no better than worthless clutter. If remodeling is impossible or too costly, and the hallway too narrow to widen with mirrors and pictures, avoid this house. It will only bring unhappiness.

99. Small foyer with a wall opposite the front door.

It's amazing how the human psychology gets agitated and tightens up in preparation for a struggle, when first confronted by an obstacle. Perhaps it is less amazing, and certainly sad, how the human psychology begins to despair, when confronted by the same obstacle time and time again. Though it may seem that a blank wall opposite the entrance to the home or even the entrance to a room may seem innocuous enough, truth is, to the subconscious it is an obstacle to one's forward progress, forcing us to turn either right or left. Furthermore, the appearance of a blank wall before us forces us to turn within. This may be appropriate when we wish to meditate or be self observing, but can be depressing and undermining to one's self confidence and self assertiveness when continually confronted by the same obstruction. Even one's posture will begin to stoop in despair at the inability to overcome this obstacle.

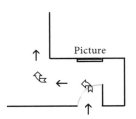

Solutions: A small foyer, with a wall opposite the front door, lowers vitality as soon as we open the door, unless, there is something to entertain the eye. Depending on how close the wall is to the door, depends on how to decorate it. The guideline is to hang a picture that is uplifting in its color and symbology, and one that gives the eye a sense of depth of field. Consider land or waterscapes that provide a distant view.

You do not want to use a mirror for this purpose, as has been suggested by more than one author. That suggestion is based on a mirror's use in "making things disappear," as it provides the illusion of looking through something. Unfortunately, a mirror at the front door operates differently. As you open the door and look into a mirror only a few feet from your face, you become startled as you suddenly see your image looking back at you. The first reaction is that of bouncing energy back at you, and with that the mirror bounces incoming qi (your good fortune/money) right back out again.

If the foyer is large enough, perhaps there could be a side table with a bowl of fresh flowers or a tabletop water fountain to energize the entrance way. Water fountains that flow in a direction are preferred to a 360° fountain. The fountain should be positioned with the water flowing in the direction of the rest of the home and not flowing in the direction of the front door. You want money flowing into the house, not away from it and you. Caution, do not install a water feature in the NE of the home until after 2024.

A small area rug is also suggested, (page 91, #97 - A Ming T'ang inside your home). Blank walls represent obstacles and give a feeling of isolation and then confusion leading to breakdowns and emotional unravelling. In short, a wall too close to the front door stifles chi flow and one's chances for growth. Tying any type of bells to your door knob that you find pleasing to hear will further energize the entrance.

100. Split wall as you enter.

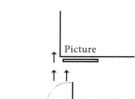

A split wall upon entering a house, such that one eye sees a wall, and the other can see either to the left or right into the home, results in a left-brain, right-brain imbalance, as one eye sees depth and the other has to adapt to a closer point of focus. The resultant imbalance lowers vitality, promotes clumsiness, undermines agility, and may contribute to persistent headaches or nerve related disorders.

Solutions: Evaluate carefully if remedies can be put in place or if the area is too tight and any remedies would add to the confusion. The challenge here is to restore balance. This can be done by either adding a plant, statue, wind chime, or other hanging decoration to bring the distant view into the foreground, or, visa versa, by hanging a framed-picture of a landscape, seascape, or some distant view covered with glass to give the illusion of depth and looking into the distance.

101. Inside beam across the hall or foyer near the front door.

Beams are not favored architectural features as they are usually weight-bearing and therefore "feel" heavy, exerting a down-pushing force. Beams also break the otherwise smooth, unobstructed qi flow across a ceiling resulting in a "choppy" flow or a life of

obstacles and barriers to overcome. As pointed out, people tend to avoid sitting under a beam (page 68, #56), and have problems sleeping under a beam (page 106, #118).

Upon walking through the front door of a home and being confronted by a beam, especially one that is fairly low, you will feel an energetic "bump" on the head. The good qi that enters through the front door will become "trapped" resulting in a feeling of depression permeating the mood of the home. Once again, if this is the only major problem, it isn't too serious. However, if this is one of many such problems related to qi flow, and therefore to cash flow, consider finding a home that is less obstructed.

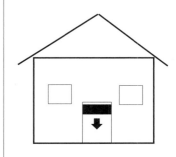

Solutions: At least paint the beam the same color as the ceiling itself. Obviously a dark color, against a light ceiling will accentuate the negative. If the beam is high enough, you might consider painting the ceiling with a *faux* finish, such as a cloud-like effect to give the illusion that the beam is not even there.

The more traditional cure for a beam is hanging two bamboo flutes somewhere along the beam to break the straight line which will alter the "down pushing" to one of "meandering." With this in mind, almost any decorations – playful masks from other cultures or hand-painted flowering tendrils – will successfully mitigate the oppressiveness of a beam, by allowing the qi to symbolically "flow through it". If the beam is low and you are tall, the illusion of making it disappear will be more difficult to achieve. Curtains, swags, corbels, and cornices are other alternative decorative countermeasures.

102. Back door or window opposite the front door.

This is an important problem that some authorities feel cannot be remedied. And often it cannot. Especially when the back door or window is in very close proximity to the front door – perhaps with only a foyer separating the two, or when the back windows are very large or sliding-glass doors.

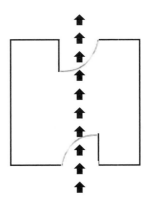

Homes that are built in this manner often have a lovely view or backyard garden to show off. In some situations, the qi can be evaluated as "captured" by the garden and sent back, but usually the qi just "flies away." Even with two rooms in between, if you can see the back window or a back door from the front door, the qi (health and money) coming in the front door tends to "race" straight through the house in the line of least resistance.

Solutions: To keep the qi from racing through the house and going out the back window or door, curtain the doorway and back window. Also consider ways to slow down or deflect the flow of qi as it comes through the front door and heads to the back of the house.

If there is a sliding glass door opposite the front door, position a potted plant behind the fixed glass side which will help to catch the eye and the qi as the front door opens and the qi zooms to the rear of the house. Placing wind chimes near the back door will also help. A properly positioned screen may be appropriate, but be careful not to obstruct the movement of people through this area. In some cases, the proper placement

of cures and the actual dimensions of the space between the front door and back door is quite adequate. In other situations, it maybe a case of using a band-aid to cover a gaping wound. The challenge is to get the nourishing qi to flow from the front door throughout the rest of the house. Be careful with this one.

Hang attractive things in the window, such as a lead-glass crystal sphere(s) to diffuse the qi. Or hang a sun catcher with pressed flowers, a stained-glass ornament, or some other attractive piece to catch the exiting qi, gather it up, and send it back to you. As you cross the threshold, you should not feel/sense your personal qi taking the "path of least resistance" and flowing out the back window. Lead-glass crystal spheres or wind chimes can also be hung from the ceiling midway between the front and back of the house.

Hollow tube wind chimes are used to conduct the incoming qi upward slowing its momentum, plus they are harmonious to hear, and even to see. Wind chimes symbolize harmony. The wind chime should be hung high enough and be small enough to be unobtrusive. How obtrusive depends on the height of the ceiling relative to the size of the wind chime and perhaps to a greater part, by the kind of wind chime you have chosen. Is it whimsical? Nostalgic? Does it have an Oriental motif? Do not use a wind chime that looks like a heavy chunk of metal that, if it fell, could hurt you as you walk beneath it.

Putting a carpet on the floor or putting a small table with flowers under the back window will also slow the qi flow down while sending back uplifting positive energies.

103. Stairway facing the front door.

Just as hallways are the internal "rivers" along which qi flows through the house, so too stairways are like "waterfalls" for qi to flow quickly down. If there is a stairway from an upper floor leading directly down to and in relatively close proximity to the front door, this will have a negative impact on health and prosperity, as you open the door and feel all the good qi upstairs flows down the stairs and out the door. This is especially so if the stairs are wood or wall-to-wall carpeted with a solid color.

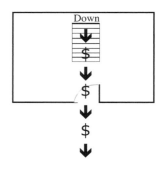

Solutions: If the stairway cannot be remodeled, so the last two or three steps face away from the front door, you can try installing as many cures as possible. Place a small throw rug between the bottom of the stairs and the front door to provide a place for the qi coming into the house to gather, and for any qi coming down the stairs to pool. It is also advisable to hang a 30mm lead-glass crystal sphere from the ceiling on a red ribbon midway between the door and the stairs, as the crystal sphere serves as a prism to defuse the qi coming down the stairs, sending it in all directions. If there is enough room, a potted plant off to the side of the bottom step will help stabilize and slow down the fast moving qi cascading down the stairs.

And my favorite, install a runner carpet with a meandering pattern to slow the qi flow down, and then, when you open the door and look at the stairs, your eye will travel up the stairs, in effect, reversing the qi flow. Hanging a large picture at the top

of the stairs, and if there is room, a small table with a vase of flowers or an attractive art piece will also assist the qi to flow upwards. Carpeted stairs also seem to make it easier to go up and down the stairs. Pictures on the wall of the stairway will also help to "lift" the qi up the stairs, while slowing the qi coming down the stairs. Though these remedies are very effective, a house with stairs directly opposite the front door is best avoided if possible.

104. Stairway going up and another going down – "Mandarin duck."

A point of focus is needed especially when we come in the front door. When the eye is greeted by a diversity of images or structural components, competing for attention, confusion results. This then is the guideline for dealing with split walls or any other entrance way situation that lacks a unified point of focus. This also includes when, upon entering the front door, you are confronted immediately by two sets of stairs – with one set of stairs going down, while the other goes up. This is said to be like a "Mandarin duck" with decorative head and neck feathers going up, while contrasting wing and tail feathers go down. Balance is thrown off, and ultimately the immune system is undermined by the stress, and the inability to rectify or adapt restfully to what is perceived, however momentarily, as a stress producing situation.

Mandarin Duck

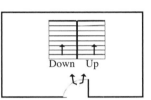

Solutions: The challenge is to create a stronger foreground to focus on. This can be achieved by hanging a large painting or art print, having a statue, or a group of potted plants. In the case of a stairway going up and another going down, you have to answer the question: Which way is the qi flowing? Then, accentuate that direction. This can be done by painting that stairwell with a brighter color, or perhaps having a runner carpet with a stronger pattern. If there is space enough between the front door and the top and bottom of the two stairways, a potted plant might be positioned to stabilize the qi flow. If there is a wall between the two stairways with enough space, a painting, print, or some other wall-hanging might draw the eye to it before the mind is split with having to make the decision to choose to go up or down. Hanging a faceted lead-glass crystal sphere and having an area carpet (page 91, #97 – Ming T'ang) would also be helpful.

Evaluate a "Mandarin duck" split-stairway situation carefully, as it can be quite critical to your focus and ultimately to your well-being.

105. Stairway at street level leads down into the main living area of the home.

Coming into a home on an upper level and then having to walk down a few steps is not as unstable when compared to walking down several, or even a whole flight of stairs. The steeper the stairway, the more uneasy the psyche feels. "What if I lose my balance?" "What if I fall?" Younger, more agile individuals are less likely to feel insecure but even those who are usually more sure-footed are likely to experience that moment of hesitation, that momentary fear of falling forward, that translates to the subconscious as unsteadiness, uncertainty, and lack of confidence. All of which correlates to the

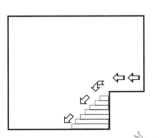

"action" of going to a lower level that may translate into a demotion, or the difficulty getting support from others.

Solutions: Evaluate how narrow, wide, high, and steep the staircase is. If you feel trepidation or even vertigo just looking down the stairs, look to buy or rent elsewhere. If the staircase isn't too steep, the ceiling is high, and the walls are set wide apart, some adjustments can be applied. Similar to a sunken living room, or any sunken room where balance is distorted, consider a runner carpet to soften one's steps and give more traction to convey firmness and certainty.

You can also put some lights along either side of the steps, as they do in a movie theater, or even a day-glo strip along the edge to clearly demarcate each step. If the stairs are wide enough, potted plants or objects on each step can also help define the height and width of the step, so the mind can quickly adjust to the descending sequence of surfaces. Appropriately positioned decorations can break up the fast, downward moving qi by giving the eye things to focus on. All these ideas can also be applied to any staircase going from one floor to another.

106. Door into bathroom by or opposite the front door.

A bathroom located immediately by the front entrance way or a bathroom door opposite the entrance way will result in great misfortune, as the qi of the house (health and money) will come in the front door and immediately go down the toilet.

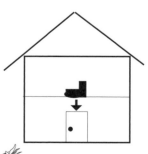

Solutions: In either case, cures need to be installed immediately, though it would probably be best to avoid homes with either of these configurations. Remember, what you see is what you get, so opening the front door should reveal a positive uplifting image, and not one of bathrooms and waste. If you cannot avoid such a home, or until you find another, at least keep the bathroom doors closed at all times.

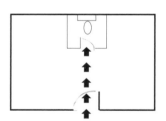

Also, it would be wise to mount a mirror on the bathroom door near the entrance to deflect the qi away from the bathroom. For a bathroom door opposite the front door, in addition to keeping the door closed, try hanging something decorative on the door, so the eye sees the decoration as the point of focus and is distracted from thinking of what's behind that door. As with any bathroom, a 30to 40mm lead-glass crystal sphere can be hung on a red ribbon between the door and where the toilet is situated.

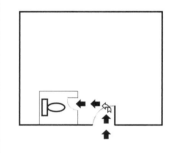

107. Bathroom above the front entrance way.

Bathroom qi is considered negative as it is associated with body waste being flushed down. The bathroom and the toilet consequently becomes a negative symbol to have over the front door of a home. Even when not thinking of the fact that the bathroom is overhead as you cross the threshold of your home, the subconscious (emotional) body "feels" the bathroom-toilet-waste-flushing imagery without a doubt. And where is the waste going once it is flushed? Find out if the pipes are plumbed to go along side the doorway possibly emitting odors or distracting sounds.

Solutions: Tough one to solve as the symbolic reality is what it is: "bathroom over doorway" – "body waste overhead." One cure is to install a mirror on the inside of the entrance way that is mounted on the ceiling with the mirror side facing upward reflecting the bathroom qi away. Some might suggest a small wind chime preferably with a pagoda on top – the kind you would have to go to Chinatown to buy – but any wind chime will do that you find aesthetically pleasing.

The wind chimes should not be too large nor too small, and not hanging so low that people might hit or graze their head. A wind chime hanging from the ceiling directly under the bathroom, will not seem obtrusive. The wind chime itself represents harmony and this situation it is the tubes that conduct qi flow upward. With this in mind, hang the wind chime to reverse the flow of negative down pushing qi, and channel good qi upward. This will bring ones' thoughts to harmony, as members of the household cross the threshold entering their abode with positive, uplifting vibrations.

108. Kitchen is the first room you see from the front door.

The first room seen gets all the attention. As mentioned in #106, the bathroom is the worst room to have next to the entrance way. The foyer with a spacious Ming T'ang is the best, and a living room the next best. The first room tends to be the one that preoccupies the thoughts of the inhabitants, especially when they come home. As a home shapes its inhabitants, even before coming home, the thoughts turn to the first room to be entered. If it is the bedroom, the desire is to take a nap. If it is a den or study, the desire is to be alone. If it is the living room and the television is visible from the door, the temptation is to turn it on. If it is stairs, the desire is to run upstairs and hide in one's room, inclining family members to feel isolated from each other.

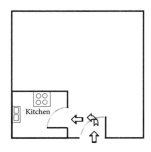

If the kitchen is near the door, thoughts most naturally turn to food. "What's for dinner?" "Is there going to be enough dessert?" "What will I have for breakfast?" If the refrigerator is in prominent view, the door will open frequently. Food issues, weight, and diet may dominate household conversations.

Solutions: If there is a kitchen by the front door, consider keeping the door closed. If there is no door, consider a curtain and some other placement of a wall-hanging or floor decoration that will draw your eye and your attention away from the kitchen and into the living area of the dwelling.

109. Stove or fireplace can be seen from the front door.

In olden days of wood burning stoves, a stove in direct line of the front door could easily be blown out or cooled by a door opening and a breeze blowing in. Though we no longer use a wood burning stove, a breeze still cools the cooking food. Perhaps more significant is the prosperity symbol of the stove and seeing it from the front door is perceived as an "attack" and therefore as a dissipation of the home's prosperity. A breeze can also cool a fire in the fireplace, but the main problem is the qi coming in and going right up the flue.

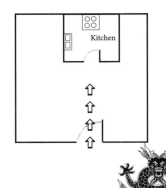

Solutions: The most obvious solution, in lieu of moving the stove or fireplace out of direct sight of the front door, is to hang a curtain or put up a tri-fold screen which offers a decorative motif to those who stand at the front door, blocking the view of the more intimate areas of family activities.

110. Entrance of an apartment next to or opposite an elevator.

With the constant activity that an elevator implies, and the on and off whirring of its motor, an apartment next to or opposite an elevator generates unstable feelings of uncertainty. Finances and health no doubt will constantly be "moving up and down." In addition to the changing circumstances of the elevator, there is also the continual distraction from the flow of people coming and going. An apartment adjacent to an elevator shaft results in even more difficulties for its inhabitants, as the noise is louder and the conscious awareness of the shaft as a dangerous place generates fears.

Solutions: Mirrors can be used to push the elevator energy away and potted plants or heavy furniture can be used as a stabilizing force. Best of all is to avoid apartments next to or opposite an elevator, unless of course the elevator solely serves your apartment.

Taiji
The balance of yin-yang opposites relative to each other,
with a little of the yin in the yang and a little of the yang in the yin,
with both encircled by Unity.

Rest, Rejuvenation, and Romance

Evaluating the Bedroom

The secret of the home and womb is one.
~~ Dennis Fairchild, *Healing Home: Feng Shui Then & Now*

The bedroom should be a place of rest, rejuvenation, and romance with a sense of security and quiet. The condition of the bedroom is more than just that it is kept clean with dusted furniture, washed windows, and a made bed with fresh sheets. The bedroom needs to be a place that feels secure so sleep is undisturbed. This means the bedroom needs to be quiet throughout the night. As a place of rest and rejuvenation, a bedroom with good feng shui is as important as having a good front door. It is best located toward the back of the house and away from busy activity where it can fulfill its purpose of providing rest along with a feeling of protection.

As others have pointed out, the bedroom is where we spend one-third of our lives. Our transitions from waking to dream realms and back again should be undisturbed, and as pleasant as possible. The bedroom should be a sanctuary, a safe haven, and a wonderful environment for intimacy and romance. A lot of thought should go into creating the best bedroom feng shui possible.

The quality of sleep is as important as the quality of our food. Just as poor quality food (containing pesticides, chemical food additives, preservatives and food coloring, or if genetically modified, overly cooked, microwaved, etc.) will undermine ones well being and result in health problems, so too, poor quality sleep will ultimately take its toll on health and vitality, which in turn will undermine relationship harmony and career success.

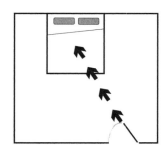

A bedroom overcrowded with furniture can be subconsciously perceived as a hostile environment – too many sharp edges and angles to battle upon entering or leaving. Even the edge of the bedroom door, if it will be pointing at the bed, should not be left partially open. Too many mirrors in a bedroom, especially mirrored closet doors, or a mirror on a dresser opposite your bed, can be over stimulating, as excessive light bounces around the room. While uncurtained windows can lack intimacy.

The bedroom needs to be a quiet place without noise with a pleasant arrangement of shapes, colors, and textures. Sleeping on a solid bed, with a good quality mattress, and comfortable pillows, surrounded by pleasant colors, shapes, textures, and images is a pre-requisite. Remove all clutter from around and beneath the bed, so qi can flow freely around you as you sleep. If the bedroom has a desk or exercise equipment, use

a screen to separate these activities from the activity of sleep. From the bed, it would also be nice to look out the window at a pleasant view of natural surroundings, especially a view of water, as this symbolizes abundance, nourishment, good luck, and inspiration.

111. Bed in the Command Position.

In evaluating the bedroom, the first and most important factor is the positioning of the bed. In considering which wall to put the bed on, there may be pre-existing conditions that limit your choosing the best arrangement. Obviously, the bed cannot be against a wall with closet doors along it.

"Placing the bed where the person trying to sleep in can't command the door makes that person feel vulnerable and unable to relax completely. Why? Because the animal body will not relax unless it can defend itself with a fair chance of success."
~~ Ralph & Lahni DeAmicis,
Feng Shui and the Tango in Twelve Easy Lessons

Solutions: Ideally, you want your headboard to be against a solid wall with the widest possible view of the whole room. This is called the Command Position.

The Command Position allows you to see the door and anyone coming through it. The Command Position also allows you to see the greatest area of the room while lying or sitting in bed without having to turn your head too far to the left or right. When you sit at your desk or lie in your bed, the Command Position gives you the greatest sense of security and, therefore, of peace and harmony.

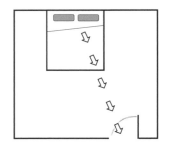

The Command Position is primarily about our ability to seeing and to anticipate what is, or may be, coming our way. Consider if you were a New York City mobster in a restaurant, would you sit with your back to the door? Probably not. It is interesting to note that when a couple goes to a restaurant, it is almost guaranteed that the man will choose the Command Position with his "weaker" friend taking the more vulnerable position of having her back to the door and being dependent on the "man" to protect her. The Command Position puts you in the driver's seat – it puts you in control of any situation.

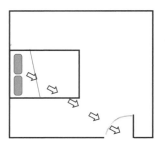

In evaluating your bedroom, if you cannot arrange your bed to be in the Command Position, consider if it is possible to position a mirror on the wall opposite the door that will allow you to see if anyone is coming in. A mirror properly placed is like a rear view mirror which keeps a driver in control by letting him or her know what's going on behind their back. Instead of a mirror, any reflective surface will suffice. Once installed, the sense of security – that is, being able to see the door and sense what is going on in the rest of the house – allows comfort, relaxation, and relationship harmony to return to the bedroom.

Mirror

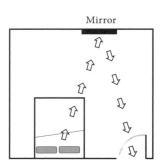

Avoid putting your bed at an angle to the wall or with a corner of the room behind the headboard. A solid wall gives the best support, while a bed floating in the middle of the room or turned at an angle to the wall symbolizes chaos and confusion. A bed positioned with a solid wall behind, with a commanding view of the largest area of the room is also the most aesthetically pleasing.

112. Door directly in front of the foot of the bed – the Coffin Position.

When the entrance to the bedroom is directly in front of the bed, it is called the Coffin Position. According to my mother, even my great grandmother from eastern

Europe had alluded to this placement of the bed as the Coffin Position. Apparently she said, "Never sleep with your feet pointing at the door to the room as that is the way they carry you out – feet first."

Avoid this placement at all costs. This situation is made worse if there is a bathroom door opposite the bedroom door, a bathroom or electronic devices on the other side of the wall from the headboard, a window directly behind the headboard, or if the ceiling is sloped over the bed, or if there is a beam overhead. Any one of these situations is detrimental and even more so if the bed itself is positioned in direct line of the door.

Death is implied by this bed position due to the continual stress of the individual sleeping with their feet to the door. A night or two or even three will not result in such a terminal fate. But certainly after years, the continual anticipation of danger, the '"what if something came crashing through the door-how can I protect myself" kind of fear and uncertainty, and the all-night activation of the "fight or flight" adrenal glands will take its toll on the immune system. This is a variation of page 78, #74 – Doorways hung at an angle – "evil door," and possibly just as severe.

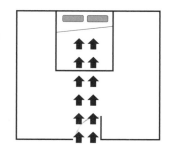

Solutions: Any solution other than moving the bed is inadequate. Temporary measures can be considered until the bed is moved; and, if the bed cannot be moved, the only solution is to move to another house.

To temporarily off-set the feelings of vulnerability, the most obvious solution is to close the door. At least this gives a moment, were the door to be opened suddenly by an attacker, to pull oneself together in time to confront the intruder. Not much time and perhaps not time enough, but at least there is a delay that may work in one's favor. In other words, there might be a little more restfulness but perhaps still too much anticipation of danger.

Some practitioners may suggest cures such as hanging a wind chime inside the room between the doorway and the bed to draw the incoming excessive qi flow upwards. Others may suggest a throw carpet between the foot of the bed and the doorway, a hope chest at the foot of the bed, and at least a footboard on the bed. Truth is, these are merely band-aids and cannot be taken seriously. Move the bed or move to another house.

Deep relaxation is not enhanced by knowing we could be taken by surprise.

~~ Nancilee Wydra,
Feng Shui: the Book of Cures

113. Doorways on either side of the bed.

Another undermining influence to avoid is a doorway on either side of the bed. Closet, garden, or porch doors are of the least importance, in comparison to the door you enter the bedroom through and the door to a bathroom. If either of these doors are on either side of the bed, health problems will soon be likely. In short, we never want to position a bed, desk, or major sitting or work area in direct line of the entrance way to a room, as that would be similar to sitting stressfully all day on a "railroad track" waiting to be "run over." In this case, it is the immune system that takes the hit.

As to sleeping in a bed with a doorway to either side, the main problem will be for the person sleeping on the side of the bed with a doorway on that side, as it will be this person who will feel more vulnerable and sleep less deeply due to the anticipation of

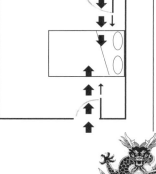

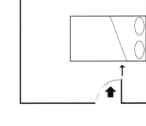

someone or something barging in unexpectedly. A doorway to either side of the bed or straight ahead translates as sleeping in readiness of an attack or having to handle an unexpected emergency. Trying to sleep while continually being prepared embattles the immune system, which needs sleep to replenish and regenerate. The nervous tension in anticipation and apprehension wears down a person's resistance thus affecting relationship harmony and personal health. The closer the door is to the side of the bed the more intense the stress, and the more severe the health issues.

The human body can handle stress for short periods of time. Like waking in the night to walk or feed a baby, but then the day arrives when the baby sleeps through the night and the parents return to normal sleep routines. But if normal is never the situation, or when stress becomes the norm, the adrenal glands keep pumping their "fight and flight" hormone, speeding up the heart beat, raising the blood pressure, accelerating breathing, and generating heightened anxiety. With this night-time stress, what else can be expected but a lower threshold of tolerance to irritating and irksome situations with ever increasing uptightness and hostile overreactions even to petty situations. If sleep is ruined, the rest of the day is a continuing disaster.

In almost everything home I have visited, it is the man who usually chooses the side of the bed that is closest to the entrance to the bedroom. Sleeping closer to the door allows the man to "feel in control" of potential emergency situations – ready and alert to protect his mate, or ready to take action if there is trouble elsewhere in the house. When the bed is in the Command Position, it really makes no difference who sleeps closest to the door, as both can sleep well. Likewise, when it comes to the Coffin Position, it makes no difference which side of the bed either partner sleeps, as both sides will be stressful.

However, when the door is to either the immediate left or right of the bed, if, as usually happens, it is the man that is in direct line of the incoming qi, invariably the man will have hypertension, while the wife, sleeping comfortably behind the man's protective readiness, remains healthy and strong. In time, he falls seriously ill of one malady or another, they might assign blame to his cholesterol or tension at work, and she becomes the caretaker to the man, as he can no longer stem the onslaught of qi that continues to flow at and over him, as he remain in readiness ever more feebly guarding the bedroom door. Until hopefully they move to a new bedroom that is more conducive to rest and rejuvenation.

If it is a bathroom door to the side of the bed, it is more likely to be the woman who will choose that side, either due to her more frequent need or the man's willingness to give the lady the convenience. (Of course an older man may also have to be closer to the bathroom if he has not been taking care of his prostate.) This situation is made even worse if the master bath is *en suite* and lacks a door that can be closed, but is connected with an archway, or a difficult, or awkward to close pocket door, which then remains open.

Though the bedroom may be considered yin when compared to the front of the house, bathroom qi is cooler and therefore yin in comparison to the warmer yang energy of the bedroom with the two not mixing very well. Sleeping is a restful, or yin, activity. People are vulnerable when they sleep and that is why the bedroom needs to be quiet and undisturbed from either outside intrusion, or intrusion from interior features such as an overhead beam, "hidden arrows" emanating from furniture, or the yin energy of the bathroom which "drains" out the warm yang energy of the bedroom.

More often than not, the individual sleeping closest to the bathroom door will soon succumb to urinary or bladder problems, or gain weight from water retention. How close the door is to the side of the bed and whether it can be closed or curtained are variables that might make this a more tolerable situation. Considering the constitutional strength of the individual sleeping near the bathroom door is, of course, one of the determining factors as to how soon before health problems manifest, or if they can be forestalled. For the most part, this is not a favorable arrangement and is one to avoid.

Solutions: The best solution is to move the bed out of the doorway. If this is not feasible, then evaluate how close to the doorway the bed actually is – five feet is very close, eight to ten feet may begin to be far enough. The only measurement tool that is dependable is your own feelings. If you can't convince yourself that you are too close or far enough away, ask a friend or family member whose intuition, or so-called feeling judgement, you can trust.

As with many situations such as this, a 40mm lead-glass crystal sphere can be hung on a nine-inch red ribbon between the entrance to the bathroom and the toilet. The crystal will diffuse the incoming positive qi and keep it from "going down" the toilet. A small throw rug can be placed between the door and the bed to slow the qi down. It is also suggested that all bathroom doors are kept closed to keep auspicious qi/money from going down the toilet. And don't forget to keep your toilet seat closed for the same reason.

As with the Coffin Position (page 100, #112), solutions, other than moving the bed to a better arrangement, are at best temporary until you find a home offering a better bedroom configuration. Needless to say, at least close the door. Unlike the Coffin Position or the entrance to the bedroom alongside the bed, with a bathroom entrance, security isn't the primary issue. In this case, a closed bathroom door keeps the warm bedroom qi from being dissipated by the cool, damp bathroom qi.

When pocket doors are awkward and hard to use, they are usually left open. To encourage closing the door, I suggest getting a draw pull or cabinet handle to attach to the very edge of the door so when it is open, the draw pull or cabinet handle keeps the door from being completely pushed inside its pocket. Then it is easy to close the door and the tendency to leave it open will be averted. If the bathroom is *en suite*, a curtain rod can be installed and curtains that can be pulled shut can be hung.

But best of all, move the bed out of the doorway. Either move the bed to another acceptable position in the room, use another room, or find another house.

114. Toilet in direct line with the bed.

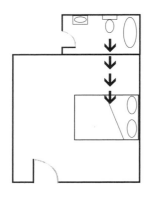

As Master Peter Leung has so astutely pointed out, the toilet itself "radiates" negative qi both forward and back. Looking at a floor plan should make it quite clear if the front or back of the toilet is in direct line of a bed, a desk or any other frequently used location.

Negative toilet qi is usually associated with ill-health, and ill-health will eventually undermine relationship harmony and/or career success. The part of the body most clearly in direct line of the toilet qi is the area of the body most likely to manifest a particular ailment, and in time the toilet qi is likely to have a detrimental effect on the immune system itself. Do not under estimate the seriousness of negative toilet qi. A toilet in direct line with the bedroom door is just as inauspicious and will also bring ill-health to those who sleep with this configuration.

Solutions: Whether the bathroom is connected to the bedroom or situated elsewhere in the house, the bed should be shielded from a toilet pointing in its direction by placing at least a 24" x 30" or 36" mirror behind or in front of the toilet to reflect the toilet energy back onto itself. The toilet with tank is usually 2 feet wide and usually less than 3 feet high.

The mirror can be positioned in the bathroom itself or on the other side of the wall from the toilet in the adjoining room. If the mirror is being place in the adjoining room, it can be placed behind a piece of furniture or in a closet – but be sure to place with the mirrored-side facing the front or back of the toilet. In the bedroom, this remedy is only necessary if the front or back of the toilet is in direct line with a sleeping arrangement. If there is a toilet in direct line of the bedroom door, find a different bedroom to sleep in. If there is a bathroom door opposite the bedroom door, at least keep the bathroom door closed and place some decorative art on the door itself.

115. Headboard on the other side of the wall from a bathroom.

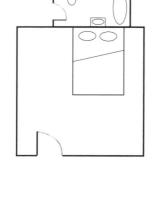

The problem with a bathroom on the other side of the wall from the headboard is how the plumbing with water in and moving through the pipes will affect a sleeping body. The most likely health complaints will also be related to the kidneys, urinary tract, or lymphatic system. If the bathroom is on the other side of the wall from the headboard, but the plumbing is not in the wall the headboard is on, the physical problems will be somewhat mitigated, however, the effect on one's psychology will still be disturbed.

Even worse is when the house's electrical system is grounded to the water pipes instead of a six foot rebar pounded down into the earth. If this is the case, then the whole house is electrified. The water pipes in the wall behind the bed become a conduit for electrical energy emanating an electromagnetic field making the water pipes in the wall behind the bed even more detrimental to health and well-being. Even without water pipes in the wall behind the bed, this is still a very negative situation as the water pipes will still be generating a massive electromagnetic field throughout the home.

Solutions: The best solution, of course, is to move the bed to a different wall. If this cannot be accomplished, as with negative toilet qi, the only real solution is to place a mirror between the headboard and the wall with the mirrored surface facing the bathroom, which should deflect the bathroom energy away from the bed. But this is another of those situations that are best avoided.

If the house electrical system is grounded to the water pipes, disconnect and have the electrical system ground to a six foot rebar pounded into the earth.

116. Electric box, electric devices, or stove on the other side of the wall from a bed.

Three case histories should help illustrate the severity of this problem. One involved a contractor who bought, renovated, and sold homes, and often lived in the homes he was renovating until he finished the work and the home was sold. This home renovator developed an arrhythmia heart condition within weeks of moving into the master bedroom suite. After it was pointed out that the incoming electrical wires were attached to a breaker box on the outside wall within twenty-feet of the headboard, he changed rooms and his heart condition disappeared immediately, much to his doctor's surprise.

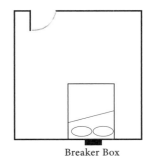

Breaker Box

Another case history is of a woman with progressively worsening cancer of the ovaries. After his wife's death from a similar cancerous condition, the woman's father decided he would be happy in the smaller guest house toward the back of the property. So he invited his daughter and son-in-law to live in the main house, thinking this would be a benefit for them having a larger house without a mortgage, and for him having his family close by.

Unfortunately, the bed in the master bedroom was in the same position as the parents' bed. On examining the bedroom, it was observed that the headboard was on the other side of the wall from the master bathroom. Although the wall had no water pipes in it, there was a wall heater with heavy electrical conduit in the wall behind the headboard. The woman's cancerous condition rapidly improved once she began sleeping in a different room. The home was eventually sold, and the couple purchased a home with a better bedroom situation. It should also be noted there was a weeping willow in the front yard near the front door, which often indicating a home with great sadness.

Electric Box
Neutralize In-coming
Electricity
with a Tri-pak

The third story is of a young couple, though very much in love, who had not slept in the same bed for some time. He regularly fell asleep on the living room couch, while she slept on the edge of their bed. Looking outside the bedroom window, I saw the electric wires from the transformer can on the utility pole stretching across their backyard to the power box bolted to the outside wall on the other side of the head-board of the side of the bed no one was sleeping in.

Solutions: Move the bed to a different room or at least do not sleep near an electro-magnetic field until you find another house. This also would include sleeping with a refrigerator on the other side of the wall, electric blankets turned on or even left plugged in the wall all night long, those little AC to DC transformer boxes plugged into the

wall beneath your head used to power telephones, answer machine, or music systems, clocks and clock radios with large red or green numbers, and so forth.

Reduce your exposure to electromagnetic fields whenever and however you can. Considering that your blood cells are like little bar magnets and are all lined up in a row as they flow through your blood stream – plus/minus, plus/minus, plus/minus. Add an electromagnetic field and the bar magnets spin around, not functioning as they were intended to function, with one consequence the undermining of the blood's ability to nourish the body by transporting vitamins, minerals, proteins, hormones, enzymes, and other components necessary for the proper functioning of the body and mind. As with other examples of sha qi, once the immune system is compromised, all kinds of strange maladies inevitably follow.

117. An irregular-shaped bedroom.

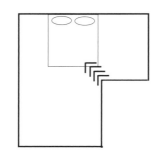

The human mind has a constant need to create order and regularity out of chaos and discord, which is why the square and the rectangle have come to symbolize regularity, dependability, and stability. A house that has an irregular shape has no easily discernible center, a front room that runs in different directions can lack focus, and likewise an irregular-shaped bedroom can make those using that room feel out of balance.

Solutions: The primary challenge is to block the "hidden arrow" coming off any corners created by irregular-shape rooms, especially if the arrow is pointing directly at the doorway, sitting area, stove, or bed. In one irregularly shaped bedroom we lived in, in addition to hanging a 40mm faceted lead-glass crystal sphere as a protection between the protruding corner and our bed, my wife covered the corner with a gossamer scarf that replaced the aggressive edge with a splash of color. Tacking up molding on the edge is another way to round the edge and transform it into a softer, less aggressive shape.

In large rooms of the house, a potted tree can also be used to block the corners of walls, pillars, or exposed structural supports. In the bedroom, plants have to be used with care. During the day while photosynthesis is operating, plants breathe carbon dioxide and exhale oxygen; but at night, the process is reversed and plants compete with humans for oxygen, while exhaling carbon dioxide.

118. Beam over the bed (compare page 68, #56 – Exposed beams and roof supports).

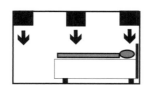

Think twice about choosing a house with beams in the bedroom and be careful about your evaluation as to the possibility of finding a true solution and not just a band-aid. Beams usually cross the bed in one of two ways: horizontally or vertically. If the beam above a bed crosses the bed from side-to-side, or vertically from corner-to-corner, the area of the body directly under will be weakened.

One couple had a beam over their bed which went over their hips and midriff. The wife had sprained her hip in an aerobics class. Nothing particularly remarkable about that except that it was already two years later and the hip was still inflamed. She had tried everything to overcome the inflammatory condition of the hip and pelvis. Con-

currently, her partner, a much more emotional type, had developed stomach cramping and was eventually diagnosed with Irritable Bowel Syndrome. This symptom also resisted the attempts of the best healers they could find. Once they understood the role the massive beam over their bed was playing in their discomfort and discontent, they covered the beam and in less than two weeks they each had complete recoveries.

Beams, if aligned vertically over the middle of the bed, will result in partners feeling separated and alienated from each other, likely ending in separation and divorce; while a beam directly over one's body as one sleeps will result in that individual feeling oppressed, and eventually succumbing to a major illness. I say this with certainty only because it has been true in every situation that I have observed and mentioned by every other teacher and in every other book: beams over beds result in serious problems.

Solutions: The best solution for beams over a bed is to cover them by completing the ceiling. This can be done with drywall, plywood or, if you like the gypsy encampment look, with fabric. As mentioned on page 68, #56 – Exposed beams and roof supports, the negative impact of beams in other areas of the house can possibly be diminished by painting the beams the same color as the rest of the ceiling.

Painting a beam the same color as the rest of the ceiling helps blend them in and upward. Using any of the *faux* finishes to create a dappled cloud-like effect can also camouflage a beam and diminish the beam's oppressive, down-pushing feeling. While beams painted a contrasting color, dark color beams against a white background or white painted beams with a dark background, accentuate the intensity of the beam's appearance.

Hanging two bamboo flutes or several decorations on the beam will alter the un-naturalness of a beam's long straight lines. Any or all of these solutions might work, especially if the beams are small and high above. Some times the only solution is to move the bed. But the best beam is no beam at all – especially over the bed.

119. Sloped-ceiling over bed (compare page 69, #57 – Sloped-ceiling over sitting area).

If the head of the bed is on the wall with a sloped-ceiling, the qi moving along the ceiling comes down rapidly, causing discomfort and giving some people chronic head-aches and others constant neck and shoulder tension.

Solutions: As mentioned on page 69, #57 – Sloped-ceiling over sitting area, it is usually adequate to hang a bamboo flute with the mouth piece down and the other end point-ing up at a 45° angle to reverse the negative influences of a sloped-ceiling. Two flutes may be stronger than one, if the slope is directly over the bed with each flute angled inward. Larger bamboo flutes with their thicker walls and notches are stronger than flutes made from reeds.

If the traditional bamboo flutes cure does not fit your interior design style, then you are challenged to find a design element that can serve the same purpose. The size

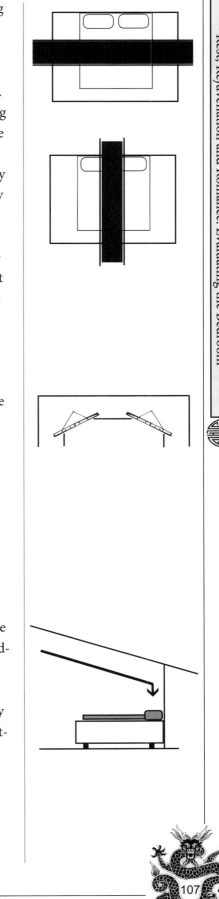

of the room and height of the ceiling also needs to be taken into consideration in evaluating the severity of the problem. Using wallpaper border trim at the bottom of the slope around the whole room can help bring intimacy to an otherwise large empty space.

Having the ceiling slope across the bed may be more difficult for the partner sleeping on the side of the bed closest to the low end of the slope, while sleeping on the wall opposite the low end may foster feelings of criticism for the partner who appears to be squashed and overwhelmed. Either way intimacy is compromised and emotional well-being undermined. Flutes or some other upward pointing objects or wall-hangings may off-set this obvious imbalance.

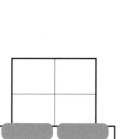

120. Bed under a window.

If the only position for the bed is under a window, rest will be disturbed by the subconscious concerning itself with the possibility of the window breaking, especially if you live in earthquake country or where the winds blow especially strong. Noises from the outside may also seem louder. A window behind a bed means no support.

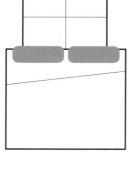

Solutions: A solid wall, like a mountain, behind the bed it best. A solid wall and a headboard provide comfort. This is another application of the Armchair metaphor discussed earlier. If there is no solid wall on which to position the bed, at least put a heavy curtain on the window that can be closed at night to provide the subconscious with its need for safety and its ability to rest without distraction. A lead-glass crystal sphere and protective images would also be helpful.

121. View from the bed into the bathroom.

Another major consideration is what each individual is seeing from his/her side of the bed. If one person is looking into the bathroom and one is looking at a beautiful view out the window or at a serene photo, print, or original art on the wall, each individual will be preoccupied with different thoughts, and the couple's conversations will reflect this reality. One will be talking about vision and dreams, while the other will talk about how "crappy" life is, moaning about life's many problems and complaints.

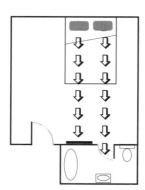

Solutions: As you evaluate the bedroom, consider if the bed will be in the Command Position without a door on either side, and if the view can be harmonious and uplifting. If one side of the bed looks into the bathroom, and the bed can not be repositioned to another wall with a potentially better view, besides keeping the bathroom door closed, consider a wall-hanging or other ways to decorate the doorway itself. How about a wall mural with the door imbedded into the design.

122. Master bedroom in front half of house, or extended out in front of the house.

The back portion of the house should be the safest, most intimate, and least disturbed by street noise, headlights, etc. A home with the master bedroom in front of the mid-line of the house can weaken a relationship. If the master bedroom, in fact, is

an extension in front of the house, this can be very detrimental to the relationship as it puts the couple figuratively, and then literally, "outside" of the house. A likely indicator the couple is headed for an inevitable separation.

 Solutions: The best that can be suggested for a master bedroom outside of the house is to position a mirror on the wall of the bedroom that would be closest to the house to symbolically reflect, or "draw," the room back into the main area of the home. Positioning of the mirror is important and might not work in all situations. In fact, a new problem can result, if the mirror will be directly behind or in front of the bed. If the mirror can be covered by the head board or off to the side of the front of the bed, this solution will work quite well.

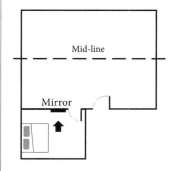

Some say it is alright to have a child's bedroom in an area of the house that extends out in front of the home, as children do come and go, and eventually will be old enough to leave your house and begin a home of their own. Others say this leaves the child feeling unprotected, certainly unconnected, and likely to feel more comfortable and at home somewhere else. A home office is well suited if located in front of the house, as it is our business connection to the rest of the world. A kitchen in front of a home encourages meals to be eaten elsewhere or on the run.

123. Bedroom over a garage.

A bedroom situated over a garage is also experienced as disturbing to one's sleep. This should be especially avoided in apartment complexes built over a communal underground garage or street level car port with many cars constantly coming and going. As with other situations, some individuals are more sensitive to these influences than others, and ultimately, it will be your own experience that will determine if this is an unfortunate place to sleep. Worst of all would be if the bed is located over the harmful electromagnetic radiation of an electronic garage door opener. These electronic devises are usually positioned in the garage close to the ceiling.

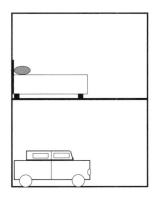

Solutions: One remedy that has been suggested is tacking a red ribbon from the ceiling of the garage to the floor of the garage and then tying a nine-inch red ribbon around the middle and making a bow. In this way, you will have symbolically connected the bedroom with the earth below. Another variable, instead of using a red ribbon from floor to ceiling, is to paint a red line from floor to ceiling, while another might be hanging a crystal on a red ribbon over each car in the garage to diffuse the negative qi. Yet another recommendation might be to put a mirror under the bed with the mirrored surface facing down toward the garage to bounce the negative garage qi away. But remember, the gaseous, toxic auto emissions will not be neutralized by crystals, ribbons, or visualizations. Of course the problem of noise or toxic emissions will not be too much of a problem if the cars are rarely used.

The problem, however, will be increased if you live in an apartment directly over a communal garage with many cars going and coming, and where tacking up ribbons

and hanging crystals may not be feasible. If you do live in an apartment complex built over a communal garage, at least avoid any apartments directly over the entrance into the garage, and if you can not find an apartment above another apartment, at least try to choose an apartment where there is the least amount of comings and goings. Tying the bed down with a rock hanging from the rope, or having heavy items in the room may also help.

124. Inadequate space to walk on either side of the bed.

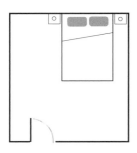

Often I am told that a prevailing health consideration is an inflamed hip or pelvis. Upon examining the bed placement in the bedroom, the reason becomes quite clear. Upon arising from the bed, there is not enough room to walk comfortably around to the front of the bed. The narrow squeeze necessitates a sideways "scooting" motion that puts extra pressure on one side of the body, compressing the hip joint causing inflammation, undermining that side's strength until eventually it buckles.

Solutions: Though the actual sprain may have happened at an aerobics class, playing tennis, or dancing at a party, the underlying cause can usually be found in the home. If the bed is oversized for the room, get a smaller bed. If there is too much furniture for the size of the room, remove some of it. Sometimes it is easier just to move the bed a foot or two further from the wall to provide adequate space for the person, sleeping on that side of the bed, to be able to get up and walk comfortably.

125. Bedroom equality.

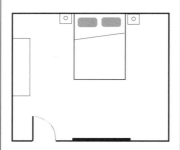

In addition to placement of the bed with a solid wall behind for support and a commanding view of the room and doorway, the bedroom should also be evaluated for satisfying other requirements to ensure calm restful sleep and relationship intimacy. One of these features is equality for both sides of the bed. This includes tables and lighting, space on both sides for equal ability to go to the bathroom, or to leave the room for whatever reason.

Intimacy will also be diminished if the room is too vast or if the bed and furniture are oversized and it is difficult to move around. It is especially difficult if either partner has a narrow space to walk along to get to the front of the bed, has to stumble over laundry, piles of books, and magazines, or has to avoid bumping into sharp-pointed edges of furniture. Any or all of these difficulties make for great obstacles to overcome throughout the day and often result in complaints, disparaging remarks, and overall unhappiness.

What each partner sees from their side of the bed is also of great importance. As mentioned on page 108, #121, if one partner is looking into the bathroom while the other has a beautiful view out a window or is looking at a beautiful, up-lifting picture or arrangement, the conversation of each will reflect the view. One will be talking disapprovingly while focusing on the problems while the other will be talking about beauty and how wonderful life is. It doesn't take a rocket scientist to know which partner

will be talking about what.

It is also very difficult to attract or keep a relationship, if one side of the bed is close to or totally up against a wall with no way for the person next to the wall to easily get out. Climbing over the partner or scooting down to the end of the bed will work for a while, but eventually the person who is "up against the wall" will want to live elsewhere. Bed situations like this usually represent a relationship that is falling apart or already has. More often then not, a bed up against the wall indicates a person who is sleeping alone as their partner seeks a more comfortable and compatible bedroom to have a relationship in – where they don't feel so constrained and where they "have room to move."

Solutions: Remember, in choosing a house, choosing the right bedroom is of great importance. So make sure you choose wisely. As stated, choose a bedroom that offers a solid wall behind the bed, no doorways to either side, adequate room to walk on either side, and one that provides a nice view or at least the space to hang uplifting images. Choose a bedroom that allows each side to enjoy equality.

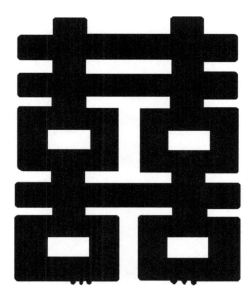

Double Happiness
The stylized Chinese character for "happiness" doubled.

Other Rooms to Consider

Kitchen, Dining Room, Child's Room, Home Office, and Garage

Feng shui…is a method of helping ourselves and others
to live according to the Way of heaven
so that universal harmony will be preserved.
~~ Eva Wong,
Feng-Shui: The Ancient Wisdom of Harmonious Living for Modern Times

• **Kitchen:** In some homes, the kitchen is the primary center of family activity: sharing meals, grabbing snacks, a place for the kids to do homework, late night conversations over a cup of tea, and one of the principal gathering places when entertaining guests.

126. Well-lit kitchen with plenty of room, or narrow and dark.

Narrow galley way kitchens tend to be less used and less inviting. Narrow kitchens tend to be good for boiling water for tea or coffee, grabbing a fast meal or a late night snack. A poorly lit kitchen is just uninviting. With a doorway on either side they are "passage ways to somewhere else" and not a source of nourishment. Nor are narrow kitchens favorable for attracting or maintaining relationships, and relationships that do exist will tend to be disturbed by bickering and discord. This is especially true if the stove is opposite the sink or refrigerator (page 114, #128). A roomy, well-lit kitchen is nurturing to the body as well as to the soul.

Solutions: The best kitchen, therefore, is light and cheery, comfortable to move around in, and easy to keep clean. The best kitchens have adequate drawers and cupboards, and perhaps a walk-in pantry.

Attempts to enliven a kitchen might be done with a cheery, canary yellow paint, or flowery wallpaper, wallpaper trim, or ceramic tile. A kitchen can also be highlighted with a decorative floor mat in front of the sink and stove, a 40mm faceted lead-crystal sphere hanging from a nine-inch red ribbon, or if the ceiling is low, a three-inch red ribbon. Keep knives in drawers and avoid using the sink as dish, glass, and silver storage.

The smaller the kitchen, the more important it is to brighten it with light color paint, pleasant decorations, and to maintain it by keeping it clean and clutter free.

127. Cook in the Command Position.

As with the position of the bed in the bedroom or an office desk and chair in the office, it is difficult to be relaxed and focused if you are anticipating someone might be suddenly coming up behind you. In the kitchen, the cook also needs to be able to see the door from wherever he or she is working. This will be easy from some work stations, while the proper placement of a mirror will make this possible from other places.

"If the cook is feeling vulnerable and tense the entire time they're cooking, when they bring the meal to the table, they might as well ask "How would you like your tension tonight?"
~~ Ralph & Lahni DeAmicis,
Feng Shui and the Tango in Twelve Easy Lessons

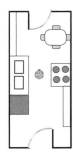

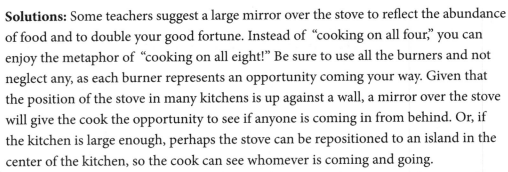

Solutions: Some teachers suggest a large mirror over the stove to reflect the abundance of food and to double your good fortune. Instead of "cooking on all four," you can enjoy the metaphor of "cooking on all eight!" Be sure to use all the burners and not neglect any, as each burner represents an opportunity coming your way. Given that the position of the stove in many kitchens is up against a wall, a mirror over the stove will give the cook the opportunity to see if anyone is coming in from behind. Or, if the kitchen is large enough, perhaps the stove can be repositioned to an island in the center of the kitchen, so the cook can see whomever is coming and going.

Remember, a happy cook cooks happy food which makes everyone happy, and happy equals rested, nourished, and healthy. Happy people go out into the world and make happy money to bring back to keep the household happy. "Happy" can also mean prosperous and harmonious. To enhance the area in front of the stove, hang a small wind chime or 40mm faceted lead-glass crystal sphere to uplift the cook's energy.

128. Stove opposite sink, refrigerator, or dishwasher.

In houses where the stove (Fire Qi) is opposite or next to a sink, refrigerator, or dishwasher (Water Qi) arguments are likely, as Fire and Water are in conflict. If the kitchen is large enough, the arguing may be tempered but in most kitchens with the Fire opposite the Water the arguments will be out of control. Though an island stove may put the cook into the Command Position, this is not so good if it is opposite the sink, refrigerator, or dishwasher.

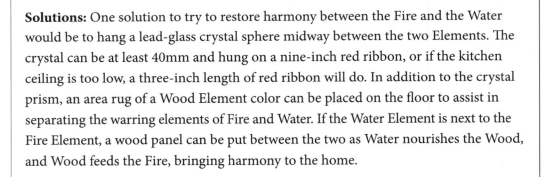

Solutions: One solution to try to restore harmony between the Fire and the Water would be to hang a lead-glass crystal sphere midway between the two Elements. The crystal can be at least 40mm and hung on a nine-inch red ribbon, or if the kitchen ceiling is too low, a three-inch length of red ribbon will do. In addition to the crystal prism, an area rug of a Wood Element color can be placed on the floor to assist in separating the warring elements of Fire and Water. If the Water Element is next to the Fire Element, a wood panel can be put between the two as Water nourishes the Wood, and Wood feeds the Fire, bringing harmony to the home.

129. Window behind the stove or stove next to the back or side door.

Positioning of the stove is also important. In olden days the stove was kept hot by throwing logs into the fire. If a cold wind or even a warm breeze blew into the mouth of the stove, the fire would be cooled and possibly put out. The meal could possibly be ruined. Even today in this modern world, the emotional identification of the stove as a source of nourishment will affect our everyday activities if something isn't quite right.

Though it is unlikely that anyone, except for a few people living quite remote, uses wood burning stoves, the vast majority of people in modern times use gas or electric (page 136, #155 – Get rid of the microwave), and a breeze blowing can affect the proper cooking of the food. The real problem however is that the subconscious interprets the wind blowing over the stove as blowing prosperity away.

Solutions: As the stove is a symbol of prosperity, it should be kept clean with all burners working properly, and it should be situated in a safe, secure area of the kitchen.

130. Bathroom directly above the stove.

As with a bathroom over the home's front entrance (page 96, #107), a bathroom directly over the stove, is another negative metaphor of loss of finances and possibly of health, as the stove is another important symbol of health and prosperity.

Solutions: Often there are cupboards above the stove enabling you to put a mirror on top of the cabinet to deflect the second floor bathroom energy away from the stove. If there is no cupboard, consider taping a small oval mirror to the ceiling directly above the stove with the mirrored surface facing upward.

• **Dining Room:** A dining room table is a place the family comes together, when in chaos, like any room in chaos, indicates lifestyles that are frenetic with the constant feeling of being overwhelmed by all that needs to be done, and all that hasn't yet been done.

131. Dining room table positioned between two doors.

Qi flows rapidly between two open doors which are opposite each other, making it uncomfortable to sit at a table situated between the two doors. Such a situation is not conducive for the family sitting together. Dining room tables located between two doorways tend to be used only on special occasions or formal occasions. Whether for every day family meals or formal occasions, family members or guests will leave the room soon after the meal is finished, or sit and squirm until permission is given. When not being used for meals, dining room tables between two doors are often used as a catch-all for whatever is coming in or going out of the house (mail, groceries, library books, etc.) and for incomplete projects in progress, as the large table becomes a great place to pile stuff.

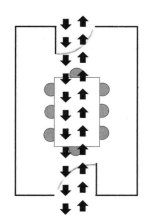

Solutions: Unless at least one of the dining room doors can be kept closed, all you can do is make a concerted attempt to resist the temptation to let chaos take over the dining room table, so that it can be maintained as a symbol of nourishment and civility.

• **Children's Room(s):** It is not uncommon for parents to rent or buy a home without considering the feng shui needs of their children. Whether the child gets their own room or has to share a room with a sibling, parents often see the child's room as a space "they will get used to." And yes, just like any growing "thing," they will learn to adapt, compromise, and compensate in order to survive, and make do with what they have. However, if we want children to develop in a truly healthy manner, both emotionally and physically, we have to provide them with not just the best educational opportunities, but also the best bedroom feng shui as possible, so that they will develop not just a balanced personality, but a strong individuality as well.

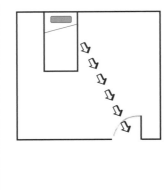

132. Child's bed in the Command Position (page 100, #111 – Beds in the Command Position).

Children are usually so tired from a full day of activity that they seem to sleep anywhere. But they sleep better if their bed is in the Command Position of the room where they can see the entrance of the room, but are not in direct alignment of either the entrance (page 100, #112 – Coffin Position), a bathroom door or other door in front of, behind or alongside of the bed. Beds in any of these unfortunate positions will result in the child getting frequent colds, allergies, or other maladies.

133. Child's bed with the headboard against a solid wall with space for qi to flow around the front and on both sides.

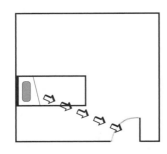

It is not uncommon to find the child's bed pushed sideways up against a wall with the intention to maximize the play space in the center of the room. Though play space is beneficial, a bed placed sideways against the wall stunts the development of the child. Like a plant on a table near a window, growth becomes one-sided, until you turn the plant and allow the other side to receive the energizing rays of the sun.

Until 6 to 7 years of age, a child can benefit from the womb-like protection of a partially enclosed sleeping space. But as a child "expands" into the world, self-worth and the ability to "reach out" to others needs to be encouraged. If the left side of the bed is up against the wall, the child's self-worth and self-confidence will become an issue. If it is the right side of the body that is up against a wall, the child's ability to reach out to others will be inhibited.

Solutions: Having a bed with the headboard against a solid wall is as ideal for a child as it is for adults, and is to be preferred. If the room is too small for this arrangement, at least move the bed six to twelve inches from the wall to allow the qi to flow on both sides and still be able to enjoy the benefits of maximum play space in the center of the room.

134. Child's desk in the Command Position.

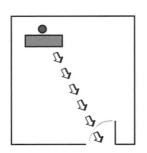

Children are easily distracted and even more so, if their desk is in direct line of the entrance or against the wall with their back to the entrance to the room. Once again, though these arrangement are often a convenient attempt to maximize play space in the center of the room, fact is, a child who can't see the door from his desk will rarely sit at the bedroom desk, curious to know what's going on elsewhere. Instead, the child will do homework at the kitchen table in an attempt to feel part of the family activity.

Solutions: Turn the desk around so the child can see the door, yet not be in direct line of the door, so he or she "knows" what's going on in the main part of the house. In this way, the child will not feel excluded. Of course, teenagers often want to close the door to their room, so they can feel they have privacy and feel secure no one is watching them as they do teenager things. But even for teenagers with a desk up against a wall,

with their back to the door, there will still be a nervous insecurity. As for an adult in a similar situation, if the desk cannot be turned around, the simple cure is to mount a mirror on the desk, wall, or adapted to sit on top of the computer monitor.

135. Large windows in the children's room.

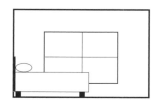

Windows and doorways can have different associations. In some cases, a doorway is like a "mouth" with the front door being the "mouth of qi." Windows are like the "eyes" of the house. Another association is that doorways are the "voice of the adults" living in the home, while the windows of the house represent the "voice of the children." Large windows in a child's room consequently can be a problem, as large windows stimulate the child to speak with a "loud voice."

Solutions: If remodeling is possible, this would be best. But at least curtains can be hung on these windows to scale them down to a manageable size. Pull-up shades can also help regulate the over stimulating qi flow from large windows.

136. Beam over a child's bed or desk area (page 106, #118 – Beam over the bed).

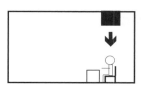

Children are no different than adults when it comes to feeling uncomfortable and insecure sitting or sleeping under a weight-bearing beam. All through the night, the child will wiggle and squirm in an attempt to get out from under it. Whether imaginary or real, sleeping under the compressed qi beneath a beam often results in repetitive illnesses, and possibly even repeated accidents.

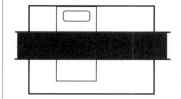

Solutions: Cover all beams directly over the bed with fabric or finish the whole ceiling with drywall or plywood. Roof supports can sometimes be painted with *faux* finishes or cloud-like patterns to blend the roof supports into the ceiling and thereby lift it up. Otherwise, hang two bamboo flutes and other decorative objects on the beam to alter its unnatural straightness and create a meandering pattern. Children's art is often the perfect solution for many feng shui problems.

137. Sloped-ceiling over a child's bed or desk area (page 107, #119).

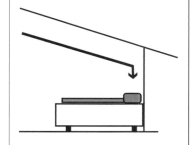

As with a beam over a bed, a sloped-ceiling can be disorienting as the mind feels most comfortable with symmetry, and a sloped-ceiling forces the brain to compensate in an attempt to maintain balance.

Sloped-ceilings can be especially difficult if the child's room is a converted attic or crawl space, with a peaked roof, or radical incline and very little wall space between it and the floor of the upstairs room. At first, this may seem fun, like a hideout, especially when the child is young and shorter in stature than when a teenager, who begin to be "shaped" by this awkwardly contorted, constricting space.

Solutions: As with the overall philosophy of feng shui which states that a home is a container that shapes the inhabitants, so an irregularly shaped room, whether distorted

by strange angular walls or a pitched roof, will equate to dysfunctional mental and emotional development.

138. Child's room upstairs and the parents' room downstairs, or child's room toward the back of the house and the parents' room toward the front.

As with a house uphill from another (page 59, #47 and page 59, #48), or even with bunk beds, the one on top will try to "lord it" over those below. Children who live upstairs and the parents down, or children in the back and the parents toward the front of a home, are children who assume control of the household affairs, as they relate to the child's needs, expectations, and perhaps, demands.

Solutions: As with page 59, #47 – House uphill from another on the same property, it is important for the property owners to retain authority over their property. So too in a family, it is important for the parents to maintain parental authority over the children. The same remedy can be applied using a photo of the parents without child. In this case, put a picture of the parents in the back left corner of the child's room, and symbolically take back the control of the household. And continually remind the child(ren) to say "please" and "thank you", and that it is unacceptable to treat the parents like servants.

139. Each child has their own space.

If there is more than one child, each needs to have their own space with a place to keep their clothes, their special toys, and an individual bed.

Bunk beds are another attempt to maximize a child's play space to the psychological detriment of the children involved. As with one house being uphill from another, the residents of the uphill home will tend to "lord it over" those lower down the hill. The human inclination to establish a pecking order seems ingrained in the human social psyche. Bunk beds seem to reinforce this inclination with the child on the upper level dominating the child on the lower level.

Another thing that continually surprises me about homes with bunk beds is how infrequently either parent takes the time to get in the lower bunk bed to assess the situation. Often when I get into the lower bunk bed to check the feng shui, I look up and see the under side of the upper bunk bed with springs, wires and mattress markings.

Solutions: If you have no alternative to using bunk beds, at least decorate the underside for your child, or help them decorate as they want. Help them create a pleasant sleep environment by avoiding over-stimulating colors and images of action figures, circus scenes, or any other imagery that is anything but restful. The theme should be calm, peaceful, and dreamy.

There are not too many solutions for establishing equality between the two children. If bunk beds are the only arrangement possible, perhaps the child with the more dominant personality can be put in the lower level in order to give the child with a milder disposition a slight advantage.

• **Home Office:** As more and more individuals work from their home, the status of the home office from a feng shui perspective is becoming increasingly important. By home office, I do not mean a desk that is used occasionally for checking e-mail or writing checks and stamping envelopes, but rather an integral part of an individual's everyday labors that bring personal income in to use in fulfilling the family's needs.

140. Home office large enough.

Home offices are frequently stuck in the corner of a kitchen, a hallway between rooms, or wherever else adequate space can be carved out. This may be adequate for answering family correspondence, signing checks to pay bills and arranging the child's after school activities, but a claustrophobic small room with no room to move (breathe), or situated in a distracting thoroughfare of household activity, is unlikely to be an office reflecting financial and creative success.

Solutions: If you are expecting to earn a decent living and enjoying the work you have chosen to do, choose a home with a room that can be set aside to be the office. If the work you do is dependent on your contacts with the outside world, a front room is best as a back room encourages reclusiveness.

If the room is small, avoid the temptation to build upwards, as high shelves with books or supplies on the uppermost shelves will cause you to have an underlying worry and concern about "what if they fall" – so keep the office shelving no higher than your head when you are seated, and preferably even lower than your shoulders. Perhaps keep office supplies and infrequently used books and files in a storage closet where they are easily accessible.

It is also important to avoid surrounding yourself too closely with sources of electromagnetic radiation. Keep as many electrical devices as possible elsewhere in the room and consider wearing an electromagnetic neutralizer such as the inexpensive Crystal Catalyst® (contact number mentioned on page 56), which will neutralize whatever electromagnetic radiation you might be exposed to.

141. Quiet and an uplifting view from the home office window.

As with the view from bedroom windows, what you see is what inspires you. If your home office plays a significant part in the daily activity of earning an income, a room with a view is especially important, as disturbing views of city chaos or country views of a stagnant pond will soon dampen an otherwise creative mind.

Solutions: If working on income producing projects, and working where thought and contemplation are necessary for setting goals and evaluating progress, choose a place of business or a home office location that is quiet and with a clear view. Definitely do not choose a spot with "poison arrows" shooting at you from neighboring roof lines, utility poles, pathways, and roadways. A room off the main thoroughfare that is quiet will also be more conducive to work well done, than being bombarded by abrasive

automotive or industrial noises.

If it is not possible to find a quiet office with a view, career success can still be strengthened by hanging a painting or a print opposite your desk that allows you to feel uplifted when you look up. Perhaps it could be a picture that stimulates creativity and the willingness to take a chance. Be careful not to hang a picture of lofty mountain peaks, as the subconscious will continually be challenged to "climb" that mountain. Use only landscape or waterscape pictures that are calm and inspirational. Or a map of the world, showing all the areas you would like to expand your business to? Or how about a ship coming to port laden with cargo and other treasures?

142. Office desk in the Command Position.

In evaluating placement of beds, desks, or where you sit at the dining room table, the Command Position is always the best. The Command Position allows us to see the door, but not be in direct line of it. It is, after all, a variation of the Armchair metaphor which describes the best site for a home with a high back for support.

Imagine sitting on a chair that had no arm rests or backing. You would certainly feel unstable fighting the tendency to fall over backwards. In a relatively short time, this precarious feeling will result in nervous anxiety and a loss of focus and concentration. Replace the backing and side supports on the armchair and the feeling is one of empowerment, of being solidly in the driver's seat.

If the desk is positioned with one's back to the door, there will be great discomfort, as one constantly wonders "what's going on behind my back?" This will have terrible consequences at work as much indeed will be going on behind the back, such as backstabbing, embezzling, malingering, gossip, etc.

If the desk is positioned in direct line of the door into the room, whether directly in front or off to the side of where one is sitting, it will be difficult to concentrate on the work at hand. As anyone sitting in direct line of a door feels vulnerable, they will either continually find excuses to get up and leave, or will continually be looking to the door to see who might be passing by, or with heightened anxiety, sit in anticipation of a confrontation with whomever might be coming in. (Compare page 100, #111 – Bed in the Command Position).

Solutions: Position the desk chair with a wall behind it for support and on the wall hang a picture of a mountain or any positive uplifting image so your sense of security and or purpose will be further reinforced. If there is no other choice but to position the desk so the entrance is behind one's back, at least put a mirror somewhere opposite the door, so you can easily see it and, like a car's rearview mirror, be able to see over your shoulder and know what's going on behind you. At best, this is a temporary solution until a better office situation can be relocated to.

143. Office desk with a window behind it.

A window behind an office chair, such as the President of the United States has in

the Oval Office, weakens the focus and removes the sense of support. Of course, in earthquake, hurricane, or tornado areas of the world, this threatening reality will increase the distracting anxiety and constant feeling of vulnerability of "what if it breaks?"

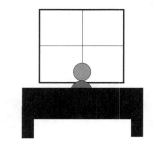

Solutions: A fellow feng shui practitioner once informed me of a photograph he saw of President John F. Kennedy sitting in the White House Oval Office, which showed an elephant sculpture on the windowsill behind the desk. In this case an elephant or tortoise would be symbolic of a "small mountain," thereby giving Kennedy support, and, in fact, he is likely to have been the most supported president (though like all presidents, had his scandalous shortcomings, which eventually were made known long after his assassination).

Indeed, any individual with a window behind his desk will feel as though he is "falling over backwards." Placing a small elephant, symbolizing a small mountain, on the windowsill, or, as is the case of Franklin Delano Roosevelt, the 32nd President of the United States, hanging heavy drapes may help considerably. A short decorative screen will also give the feeling of being supported, especially if there is an image such as a mountain to reinforce this feeling of support.

144. Toilet in direct line with the office desk and chair.

The toilet itself "radiates" negative qi both forward and back. Looking at a floor plan should make it quite clear if the front or back of the toilet is in direct line with where a desk will be positioned. The negative toilet energy is mostly associated with ill-health (page 104, #114 – Toilet in direct line with the bed). The effect negative toilet qi has on an office desk and chair is an undermining of business prosperity and opportunity. Do not underestimate this problem.

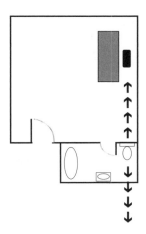

Solutions: Whether the bathroom is connected to the home office or situated elsewhere in the house, the desk and chair should be shielded from the toilet by placing at least a 24" x 30" or 36" mirror behind or in front of the toilet to reflect the toilet energy back onto itself. The mirror can be positioned in the bathroom itself or on the other side of the wall from the toilet in the adjoining room. If the mirror is placed behind the tank, it can be camouflaged by putting wood or cloth on the tank and a decorative object on top. If the mirror is being placed in the adjoining room, it can be placed behind a piece of furniture or in a closet, and be sure to position it with the mirrored-side facing the wall in the direction of either the front or back of the toilet.

145. Bathroom door opposite the office door.

Another variation of the negative bathroom energetic leading your thoughts and your success "down the drain," or getting "flushed down" the toilet. What you see when you leave your office has a strong effect on the subconscious. And bathrooms and toilets are synonymous with waste, flushing, and the opposite of where you want your thoughts to be.

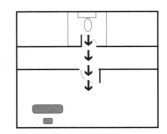

Solutions: If you get stuck with a bathroom door opposite your office door or any other frequently used door of the house, affix a mirror to the outside of the bathroom door to "bounce" the auspicious qi away. If you hang a mirror, be sure to hang it securely, so it doesn't generate a need to worry about "what if the mirror breaks" if the door is closed too hard.

Frameless mirrors can be hung with mirror hangers in all corners. A framed mirror can be hung on a wire but then earthquake putty (sold at most hardware stores) can be pressed on each of the lower corners to secure it tightly. Other decorations can be considered such as framed-pictures with landscapes or other scenes that give a sense of depth, while the glass over the picture reflects the good qi away.

• **Garage:** If the garage is a separate structure, how the garage is utilized is less important than when it is attached to the main house. In many modern single dwelling homes, not only is the garage attached, but there is a door connecting the garage with the rest of the house – sometimes through a utility room and sometimes directly into an important room such as the kitchen.

146. Garage large enough for cars, storage, or other uses.

It is quite common for a home-owning family to have at least two cars and the need for extra storage or living space. Choices have to be made. Turn it into a family room, extra bedroom, or keep it for cars and storage? Garages are sometimes the only place to locate the washer-dryer, and even an extra refrigerator. Garages can be busy places.

Solutions: With growing families, garages often get chaotically overloaded, as they try to serve multi-purposes. If the garage is also needed for exercise equipment, workshop, or teenage drum rehearsal space, consider a three car garage.

Social conditioning seems to dictate that the garage is under the rulership of the man of the house, just as the kitchen is most typically the domain of the wife. Be that as it may, whoever holds sway over the garage, needs to keep it organized, as the garage is a place of transition between the outside world and the world of the home. Storage closets are best, but if you use open shelves consider installing curtains that can be closed to cover the chaotic appearance of the various household items that are likely to end up being stored in the garage. Though you may not decorate the garage to look as beautiful as your master bedroom, nevertheless, do not let the garage look trashed out and neglected either.

Section III

Additional Feng Shui Secrets Ancient & Modern

Understanding Your Self

Knowing ourselves
leads to understanding the world
around us, and in turn, knowledge of the world leads
to greater understanding of the self.
At a very deep level,
the Feng Shui of an environment
has the power to support our search
for self-realization and outward expression.
Surrounded by harmony, we are aided in achieving balance
for ourselves and for those whose lives we touch.
When we look up at the clouds,
or feel the soil between our fingers,
we are ultimately examining our own souls.
~~ Dr. Baolin Wu and Jessica Eckstein,
Lighting the Eye of the Dragon: Inner Secrets of Taoist Feng Shui

Double Happiness

Wealth and Partnership Areas of the Home

The 3-Door Bagua Template

Remember: Your home mirrors your life and the energy patterns
that you send out to the world. Try to decode the messages
that your energy is sending out, for hidden in those signals
is another aspect of who you are,
waiting to be embraced, acknowledged, and transformed.

~~Nancy SantoPietro, *Feng Shui: Harmony By Design*

Where we live, like everything we choose to do, and everything we attract to us, no matter how unwittingly, is a reflection of who we are. As the renown psychologist C. G. Jung stated: "Until you make the unconscious conscious, it will control your life and you will call it fate." As we evolve toward an integrative sense of wholeness, it is important to understand that neither our joys nor sorrows happen to us arbitrarily. It is only by observing and examining our actions and thoughts, and the circumstances of our life, that we can see what changes are needed for self improvement. Whether consciously acknowledged or buried deep in the unconscious, as the late great Charlie Butterfly once said: "If it is happening to you, it is happening for you."

Just as one's handwriting, numerology and astrology can be analyzed to reveal one's personality, beliefs and expectations, so too, the kind of feng shui problems or benefits a home has tells the story of who we are and how we live our lives. We just need to know how to "read" the story that it tells. If the home is like a container shaping the content of those living within, if we can change the container in positive ways, it stands to reason that the lives of those living within will also be improved. As to those feng shui problems we are not able to resolve, at least we can attempt to minimize their negative impact. Whether resolvable or not, first we have to identify the problem. Once the problem is identified, then we can determine the seriousness of the problem and what, if anything, we can do.

Thus far, in our search for feng shui problems needing solutions, we have relied heavily on the principles and concepts of Landform Feng Shui. As explained on page 12, Landform Feng Shui is the most fundamental approach to feng shui and the foundation upon which all other approaches to feng shui depend on for their efficiency and effectiveness. Landform Feng Shui is an approach that utilizes nature imagery to examine the actual physical influences of the home or business environment – house site, property shape, structure, bed and desk relationship to toilets, windows and doors, and so forth. All situations that influence how the qi flows to and through what we call the "external and internal landscape" of the house.

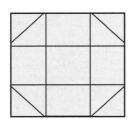

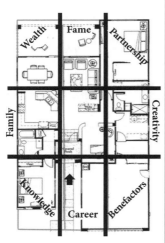

Bagua Template on a House Floor Plan. Arrow shows front door in the Career Gua.

Another powerful technique we can use to evaluate the strengths and weaknesses of any size structure, a specific room, or a property with clearly defined boundaries, is the Bagua Template (pron.: *bah-gwah)*. The Bagua Template is a diagnostic tool that gives us insight into how we, consciously or unconsciously, project our hopes and fears onto our living and working environments. It also gives us insights into those areas of our life that most need improving, That is, the Bagua Template in another way we can "read" the story of any space, as that space reflects the strengths and weaknesses of those living or working within.

The Bagua Template

The Bagua Template is an octagon shaped diagrams. As in the illustration to the left, if we lay this eight-sided diagram onto a square floor plan, there is four actual sides and four corners arranged around a center box. Though the eight-sided Bagua Template has many uses in feng shui, acupuncture and martial arts, a more recent application for how we can divide a space into nine equal boxes, was developed by Prof. Thomas Lin Yun, the originator of the Black Sect Tantric Buddhist School of Feng Shui (see page 149). This innovative application, referred to as the Bagua Map or 3–Door Bagua (illustration next page top), over the years has proven to be yet another dynamic approach to analyzing, or 'mapping,' a given space, and of telling the story of that space.

The Eight Life Aspirations

As can be seen in the illustrations (left and next page top), each side of the Bagua is assigned a different life desire, or aspiration. These are life desires shared by all humans, regardless of culture, ethnicity, education, or profession. With some variation these aspiration have been universally recognized as concerns common to all people, during all the thousands of years humankind has populated planet Earth, and regardless of where on planet Earth humans have lived.

As will be explain below, the placement of each Life Aspiration on the Bagua is based on how the human mind subconsciously projects these Aspirations onto a given space. With some variations these Life Aspirations are: Wealth/Abundance, Fame/Reputation, Love or Business Partnership, Creativity/Children, Benefactors/Travel, Career, Knowledge/Academics/Spiritual Path, and Family/Community. The Center section is often labeled Health, and also represents everything else not already included.

Aligning the 3-Door Bagua with the Mouth of Qi

After superimposing the nine boxes of the Bagua Template onto a floor plan (left), or on a site plan, where each Aspiration is located is based on how we enter the space. As depicted in the illustration (top next page), we align the Bagua with the wall the entry door is on. This means the house is entered through the Benefactors Gua, the Career Gua, or the Knowledge Gua. It is for this reason three doors are shown, and hence the name, 3-Door Bagua to differentiate it from other ways the Bagua is used.

[continued on page 128]

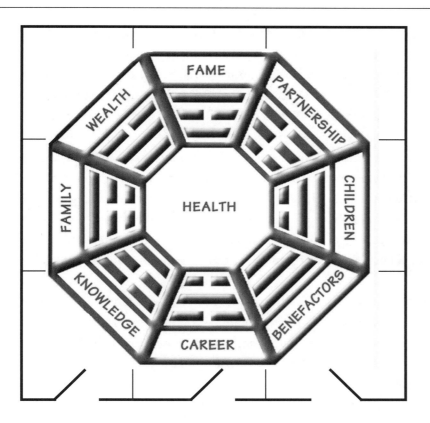

3–DOOR BAGUA

The entry way into the house, room or onto the property determines
the location of each of the Eight Life Aspirations.

Note for Feng Shui Students:

The Bagua Template has many applications in Chinese metaphysics. In Chinese *ba* means "eight" and *gua* means "symbol." The "eight symbols" referred to are the eight Trigrams, which are eight combinations of divided yin (— —) and solid yang lines (——). Each Trigram is assigned a side of the Bagua, and each is associated with a different set of attributes. Throughout history the Bagua has been used in a wide variety of ways from explaining Taoist cosmology to their subtle use in Acupuncture, Qi Gong internal exercises, as an essential tool used in the various Compass School approaches to Feng Shui (see page 148), and even as a protective talisman (see Note page 48 top). Combined with each other in all possible combinations, they generate the 64 Hexagrams of the *Yi Jing*, or *Book of Changes*. The Bagua, Trigrams, and Hexagrams of the *Yi Jing* date back to the Bronze Age Shang Dynasty, 1600 to 1046 BCE. (Note on transliteration: Alternatively, some books use the Wade-Giles spelling *Pa Kua* instead of the Pinyin *Bagua*, and the Wade-Giles transliteration *I Ching* instead of the modern Pinyin *Yi Jing* spelling.)

Eight Trigrams

Bagua Mirror
with Early Heaven
Arrangement of Trigrams
Used to Bounce Away
Negative Qi and Attract
Auspicious Qi

Bagua and Taiji
with Later Heaven
Arrangement of Trigrams
Used as a Talisman to
Protect from Negative Qi

This approach is best explained by the Theory of Relativity, as applied to the concept of how an observer's perception of an environment changes as the observer's point of view changes. Prof. Lin Yun labeled this use of the Bagua, the "Compass of the Heart" approach, as it reveals how we intuitively associate different Life Aspirations to different areas of a structure relevant to where the entryway is and how we enter that space.

To help us understand how each Aspiration is assigned a location, we need to understand an even more basic way we can divide our living or work spaces – front and back, and left side and right side. The front is considered more yang and active, the back portion is more yin and passive. The left side of the home is seen as a projection of our more aggressive, linear, masculine left side of our brain, while the right side of the home reflects the more receptive, intuitive, feminine right side of the brain.

"Mapping" a floor plan in this way, the more protected, back left side of the home is more naturally considered as the "stronghold" of the home. Therefore, we associate that section with the Wealth or Abundance Gua in comparison to areas near the more vulnerable to intrusion front door. Likewise, the back far right side, being a projection of the more sensitive and intuitive right hemisphere of the brain, corresponds more naturally to the Partnership Gua. This area of the dwelling is also more secure and undisturbed, in contrast to being near the front door, where it would be more vulnerable and less intimate.

The psychological implications are quite clear; if there is trouble at, or danger coming in the front door, the further we are from the front door, the more opportunity we have to decide on how to deal with the situation – basically, either to confront it or run. Using the Bagua Template to divide a property site plan, house, or room floor plan into nine areas, is a convenient method to organize our association with these human desires, or Life Aspirations.

Applying the 3-Door Bagua – What's Included and What's Not?

The 3-Door Bagua can be used to analyze any clearly defined space, whether a specific room or a property site plan. When used to analyze the floor plan of an individual structure, it is used to determine if there are missing corners, extensions, or other potential feng shui problems. Though the Bagua itself is eight-sided, it is not constrained in anyway as it can be stretched to evaluate any shaped structure from square and rectangle to any one of the so-called odd-shape structures, as long as it conforms to the following basic rules:

1. When applied to a structure, the only spaces included are enclosed by solid walls and windows. Based on this criteria, screen porches or attached car ports do not qualify, while a garage or a glass enclosed porch that is accessible to the rest of the house through an internal door does qualify.

2. As seen in the illustrations to the right, when the nine boxes of the Bagua are placed on an irregular-shaped floor plan, if an outside wall extends at least halfway, this will result in at least one missing Gua (see also #148 below). Conversely, if the outside wall is less than half of a side of the structure, the Bagua is not drawn on the whole floor plan, just the largest section. This results in these smaller areas being considered as an "extension," adding extra to the Gua that they are attached to (see also #149 below). This would also include bay windows, mud rooms, and any utility rooms, if they are connected by an internal doorway.

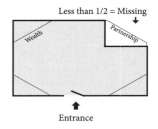

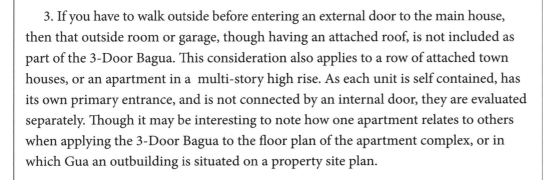

3. If you have to walk outside before entering an external door to the main house, then that outside room or garage, though having an attached roof, is not included as part of the 3-Door Bagua. This consideration also applies to a row of attached town houses, or an apartment in a multi-story high rise. As each unit is self contained, has its own primary entrance, and is not connected by an internal door, they are evaluated separately. Though it may be interesting to note how one apartment relates to others when applying the 3-Door Bagua to the floor plan of the apartment complex, or in which Gua an outbuilding is situated on a property site plan.

Multi Story Apartment Buildings

In a multi story apartment building, if one apartment is either missing a corner or has an extension, all the apartments above it and below it will be either missing the same Gua or having the same extension. And, therefore, telling the same story.

One case history stands out concerning an apartment that was clearly missing the Partnership Gua. The client occupying this apartment had moved in with her husband, and within a short time they decided to separate. When I pointed out the missing Partnership Gua and explained the implications, she informed me that the tenant before she and her now ex-husband had moved in, also became single soon after moving in. As to the predecessor history of those apartments below and above hers, she was aware that many had histories of either relationship struggles over the years or a series of men or women who lived alone. After doing the recommended remedies, the client soon met someone new with whom she remarried a few years later.

Room, House, Property, Desk

Remember, though we are primarily examining the placement of the 3-Door Bagua on the floor plan of the house, the 3-Door Bagua can also be laid out on each room of the house, and on the property site plan as well. This technique is equally as dynamic, whether applied to a single detached dwelling or an apartment on the top floor of a high rise. It can also be used in a business to determine where a cash register might go, or where the sales team would be best positioned. If you use the 3-Door Bagua to evaluate your city hall or state capitol, I am sure you will discover some interesting insights into how well your local or state government is functioning.

In establishing priorities, though we might start by evaluating the floor plan of the house for structural considerations, perhaps even more important is what the 3-Door Bagua says about a frequently used room where we spend many hours of a day, such as a bedroom or office. It is also in each room of the house that we can compensate for any weakness that may be observed in the house floor plan. For example, if we discover the house is missing the Partnership Gua, the Partnership Gua of each room can be stimulated to make up for this structural deficiency. Of third importance would be the property site map with the assignment of where each Gua is situated, likewise, determined by how the property is entered. Clearly, a dead tree in the Partnership Gua will have a major impact on the relationship harmony of anyone living on such a property.

Recently, I received a call from a client in a state of panic. Apparently, an excavation to dig up a septic system had just commenced in the Wealth Gua of the property. The owner informed me that within a few days, they suffered a series of unexpected major financial losses. I informed them that before beginning this necessary work, they needed to do a prayerful, or an attunement, meditation and place a screen between the home and the work area, even if it was just a sheet hung on a cord stretched between two trees. Once they did both their finances again stabilized. Alternatively, they could have placed a wind chime between the home and the work area. A similar approach is needed for any remodeling project to avoid the adverse effects of breaking down a wall to enlarge a room, or tearing out old cupboards and counter tops to redo a kitchen.

Wealth and Relationship Guas, Plus Six Other Guas

I have chosen to focus on the Wealth and Partnership Guas in particular because these two Guas are such essential Life Aspirations. As to the much desired Aspiration of good Health, specific to its assignment at the Center of the Bagua Template, it has already been discussed previously (see page 66, #53 – Fireplace, stairway, skylight, or bathroom in the center of the house.). Though Health is assigned to the Center of the Bagua, as the energetic Heart of the House, it should also be apparent by now that feng shui problems that can have an undermining influence on health can be found throughout the house, and that the Heart of the House, if possible, should remain open, uncluttered, and free of any negative symbolism.

Though the focus of this chapter is primarily concerned with how the structure of a house can reveal problems associated with the Wealth and the Partnership Guas, the remaining six Aspirations are also shown in the illustration. These additional Guas can also be analyzed using the same criteria with considerations for a missing corner, an extension, or a bathroom location with the solutions being much the same.

However, what each Gua reveals about the life of a home's inhabitants is more likely to be discovered in analyzing the meaning of the symbolism expressed by the choice of decorations, specific colors, textures and shapes, and how that area is being

utilized. Therefore, an analysis of what "story" all the Guas might tell has less to do with Landform Feng Shui, and more to do with interior decorating – a subject I will elaborate upon in my next book, *Feng Shui Interior Design Secrets*.

The 3-Door Bagua and Interior Decorating

Apart from the few crucial problems the 3-Door Bagua may reveal about a structure, its use as a template for Interior Design is where this technique really comes in handy. As you consider each Gua, whether on the room, the whole floor plan or the property site plan, ask yourself two simple questions: what items and images are located in each area and how do they either enhance the Life Aspiration assigned to that Gua, or how might it be detracting?

Obviously, a framed photograph of a loving couple in the Partnership Gua would be an enhancement, while a doggy bed or pile of laundry would be detracting. As mentioned at the beginning of this section, just as one's handwriting can reveal one's personality, beliefs and expectations, so too, how we decorate our homes, and the kind of feng shui problems or benefits a home has, tells the story of how we live our lives. We just need to know how to "read" the story that it tells, and, as you will continually discover, the 3-Door Bagua can be quite revealing.

147. Hill sloping down behind the house weakens the Bagua Template.

Where the eye goes, so goes one's thoughts, and consequently one's qi. As discussed previously, the ideal house site is strengthened by a hill behind the dwelling and two low rises on either side, creating the Armchair effect, and as depicted by the Four Celestial Animals. In contrast, a hill sloping down and away from behind the house is the equivalent of removing the backing of an armchair, and then constantly making adjustments not to fall over backwards. If there is no protection from behind, then you'll always feel uncomfortably exposed and insecure, as you nervously "watch your back."

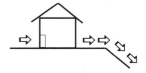

Whichever rationalization you choose to follow adds up to about the same. Either one or all three of the Aspirations of Wealth, Fame or Partnership will literally "go down hill" as you struggle to keep it together. Though there are suggested cures for this sort of a situation, the best cure is to not rent or buy a house with a hill sloping behind it. Especially if this negative factor is further reinforced by a roadway, a back door, or a bathroom in the Abundance or Partnership Area, etc.

Solutions: To offset the weakening of the Bagua by the downhill slope, the proper use of colors (gold, red, purple for Abundance; pink, white, pastels for Partnerships) and symbols related to Wealth and Partnership will do much to strengthen these Aspirations. In addition, a bright colored flag or pennant on a pole at the bottom of the slope will help "lift" the qi back up. Even stronger might be a flood light on a pole at the bottom of the slope hot-wired to the house, pointing to the roof to "shoot" the energy back to the house, whenever it is turned on. The light bulb need only be turned on once to

activate the intention of this remedy.

Recently, I was asked to assist in choosing the best house site on a sixteen acre parcel of land. Gentle sloping allowed for a few excellent house sites featuring unobstructed ocean views. The one chosen by the landowners was overlooking a gulch. Very magical with fern covered slopes, tall, gnarly trunk, robusta eucalyptus trees, and a wonderful marriage of mystery and nature's wild place. The devic energy was quite strong.

I immediately suggested they move the house away from the cliff about a hundred yards and realign the house, so the side, and not the back of the house, looked out over the gulch. With a gulch behind the home, the Wealth, Fame and Partnership Areas would have nothing to support them, resulting in the residents becoming "edgy" from "living on the edge." "Edgy" equals nervous, jittery, and short-tempered. It is difficult to feel calm, focused and secure when you are "living on the edge." (See page 29, #4 – Houses built on the edge of a cliff, ravine, or gulch.)

Not only does an upward-sloping hill behind the house provide support to these three Guas, but by putting a large deck on the side of the home facing the gulch, it allows the residents to visit the devas (nature spirits) in their wild place, rather than bringing the wild, sometimes out of control, nature energy into the home.

148. Missing Corners.

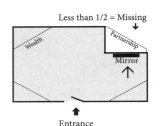

Less than 1/2 = Missing

Entrance

A missing corner is determined by measuring each side of the structure and discovering that one side extends at least half way the length of the whole house, but not all the way. The corner that is notched out of the square or rectangular-shape is referred to as a "missing corner."

Missing either the Wealth Gua in the back left corner of the home or the Partnership Gua in the back right corner can be further undermined if the property behind the house slopes downward or has a road or river flowing by. In other words, be careful in your evaluation that you can more than adequately compensate for a missing back corner of the house. Missing any of the other Guas and their associated Life Aspiration can also be troublesome, but are usually easier to compensate for.

Solutions: In many cases, this can be remedied by filling in the missing corner with a patio, landscaping, or outside features such as a birdbath or sculpture. But in many other cases, the consequence of a missing corner can be disastrous, especially if it is difficult to implement an outside patio, landscaping, etc. due to a driveway.

Mirrors can also be installed on the inside wall to give the illusion of depth and that the room extends into the missing area. Consider too that as you remedy the inside wall for the feeling of irregularity, you can also energize the two corners that have resulted from one corner being absent. In this sense you now have two Abundance Areas or two Partnership Areas.

The presence of a structural support in any of the corners may also indicate that there are problems in that area of life, as the aggressive edge "cuts" into that area of consciousness, reflecting abundance or relationship problems.

Note Well: As mentioned, the 3-Door Bagua Template can be mapped out on each room of the house, therefore, each room also has an Eight Life Aspiration layout. This makes it possible to stimulate these corners to overcome the negative implications of a home with a missing corner.

149. An overly large extension in any of the areas of the house.

An extension is determined by measuring the outside wall of a home from corner to corner. If one side extends beyond the outer wall, but is less than 50%, it is termed an extension. (A missing corner is more than 50% – see #148 above).

A slight extension is favorable as it will be stimulating to the area of the Bagua that has the extension. For example: if in the Wealth Area, it means greater prosperity.

However, if the extension is overly large, it can bring negative consequences. In the Fame Area, it can give false expectations or an inflated sense of importance. In the Wealth Area, it can give over confidence in gambling or investing. In the Benefactors Area, it could represent being let down by those who offer assistance. In the Partnership Area it could represent lack of intimacy and dysfunctional relationships.

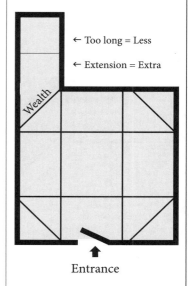

← Too long = Less

← Extension = Extra

Entrance

Solutions: To mitigate these adverse circumstances, strengthen these Life Aspirations in other rooms of the home. In the room that is over expanded, try to decorate or arrange the furniture to create more focus and a more balanced sense of proportion.

150. Bathroom in the Wealth, Health, or Partnership Areas.

Just as missing corners are not desirable, so too having your bathroom in a corner will also present a challenge. A say a "challenge" as the bathroom has to be somewhere. However, a bathroom in your Wealth Gua, and having your prosperity "go down the toilet" or "down the drain" can be very difficult to remedy.

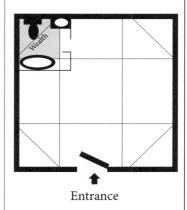

Entrance

Solutions: To overcome a bathroom's "draining" influence, at least keep the toilet seat down and the bathroom door closed. This is a good practice regardless of where the toilet is located. In fact, consider hanging a mirror on the outside of the door to deflect good qi from entering the bathroom.

Also, consider hanging a 30mm or 40mm lead-glass crystal sphere between the door into the bathroom and the toilet on a three or nine-inch red ribbon (use embroidery floss or silk cord) to diffuse the qi that does enter the bathroom.

As with a bathroom in any of the corners, appropriate colors and symbols (see Solutions, #147) can be used to strengthen the Aspiration associated with the corner under consideration and to help overcome the good qi being drained by the bathroom.

For the Partnership Area, the colors should be soft and intimate such as pink, pastels, or even white. Yellow, an earth color, can be used to absorb the water. Avoid using watery-colors (most blues and dark colors) as they will add to the dampness. In this area, you can have images of couples, whether two Mandarin ducks who are said to mate for life, two people walking holding hands, or Rodin's or Klimt's "The Kiss."

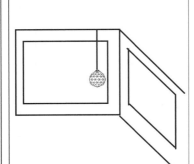

For the Wealth Area, recommended colors are warm colors, such as red, yellow, and orange, or colors associated with wealth such as royal purple. But avoid gold, as you do not want to "flush" your wealth away. Do not have any pictures of family members, so you don't "flush" their wealth away either. But the best solution is to find a home that does not have a bathroom in either Abundance or Partnership Areas.

151. Back doors or large windows in the Abundance or Partnership Areas of the home.

The home, we have said, is like a container; and like a container, a home needs solid walls, windows, and doors to hold onto whatever qi flows in. Psychologically, the corners are needed for strong structural support. Qi accumulates in corners. When the corners are two windows coming together at a right angle, qi "leaks out," and a sense of "fragility" is projected. With a "weak" far left back corner, wealth is lost, with a "weak" far right back corner, relationships are strained. This weakness is also found in homes with back doors, especially large sliding glass doors in either rear corner.

Solutions: If there are two windows, a curtain can be hung in the corner to make a solid corner that can "hold" qi. Perhaps a small table can be placed there with appropriate symbols of wealth or relationship, according to which corner is being strengthened. A 40mm lead-glass crystal sphere can be hung on a nine-inch red ribbon as an additional energizer. If it is a back door that is "leaking" energy, hang a wind chime outside the door to draw good qi in, and place symbolic items in the actual corners as stabilizers.

If a door with partial glass, cover the glass with curtains. If sliding glass doors, put three potted plants on the outside of the fixed door be sure to hang a wind chime, and perhaps some static cling window decorations or hanging sun catchers can be placed on the moving door. Whatever you do, do not block the door making it difficult to use. Remember, energy flows in both direction. Though blocking the door will keep good qi from going out, it will also be obstructing good opportunities from coming in.

152. Mother-in-law's or children's room in Partnership Area.

Ideally, the master bedroom should be toward the back of the home, regardless of which area of the Bagua Template it is in. Any room used by both partners or the family would be acceptable, if located in the Partnership Gua, such as a kitchen, dining room, or even an office. However, a child (especially a step-child), a mother-in-law, or any relative or friend in the Partnership Area can be a problem, as they will dominate the primary relationship of the household, either by distracting the couple with their pre-occupations and demands, or causing conflict in one form or another.

Solutions: It is beneficial to place a photograph of the home's primary relationship in the corner of the Partnership Area of the home to strengthen the relationship. If an actual photograph seems out of place, as may be indicated by a step-child or roommate, then something representing the couple – perhaps a gift or some item symbolic of the couple's intimacy and love – may be hung in the corner or placed on the windowsill.

Things to Change If You Can

Removing Contributors to Poor Feng Shui

Feng Shui is based on the premise that people experience happier, healthier,
more prosperous lives when their home and work environments
are harmonious. As with human bodies, the "healthier" the bodies
of our buildings are, the more they support us in living a rich,
creative and joyful existence.

~~ Terah Kathryn Collins,
The Western Guide to Feng Shui

Many feng shui problems that we encounter in examining the home can be changed without considering extensive and expensive remodeling. However, sometimes remodeling may be the best solution for removing such problems as decorative pillars or beams that obstruct qi flow. Or at least those that do not provide crucial weight-bearing support for the roof or upper floors. And, as we have seen, if we can't remove it, than at least decorate them.

Some homes come with features that are easily removed. If an apartment or house is rented, you might be able to get approval from the owner of the building to remove items or features you do not like or wish to live with. In some cases, things can be put carefully in storage, and then reinstalled to their original locations when you move.

153. Ceiling fans.

Ceiling fans, though better than air conditioning in regard to the air you breathe, still emanate an electromagnetic field from their AC/DC motors. Apart from this factor, the main problem is the "chopping" motion of the blades. The whirling blades overhead generate fear and uncertainty as the chop, chop, chop movement is felt as a threat to the subconscious, which fears these rotating blades as potentially "flying off" and hitting you. Ceiling fans directly above the head disturb the heart and nervous system as they "grind" away.

Ceiling fans that are acceptable are high above, or at least not directly above sitting areas where they "chop" the aura and crown chakra or over sleeping areas where they "chop" the legs and feet. Some ceiling fans have attached light fixtures which further add to the visual clutter, especially if you have to duck to avoid hitting your head when walking by. Ceiling fans that wobble on their stems are of course the least desirable. It probably will not fly off and hit anyone. Even though it is securely bolted to a ceiling rafter, the "what if it flies free" screams loudly to the subconscious to get out of harm's way.

Ceiling fans are relatively easy to remove and can be replaced with a low profile ceiling light fixture. A suitable substitute for the cooling aspect of the overhead fan

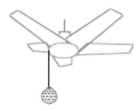

Hang a small lead-glass crystal sphere from the pull cord of an overhead fan to deflect chopping action of blades.

are floor fans such as those made by Vornado. These deep scoop fans are designed to circulate the air similar to an air conditioner. Unlike ceiling fans which remain unused dust collectors for most of the year, floor fans are easily put away and out of sight when not needed, and easily taken out when the heat of summer returns. If you cannot remove the ceiling fan, then diffuse the "chopping" by hanging a 40mm lead-glass crystal sphere from the pull cord.

154. Remove louvered windows and vertical blinds.

Remove louvered windows and vertical blinds as these straight edges emanate "hidden arrows," as they "slice" the interior space when partially opened. If there is no way to replace them, consider keeping them completely closed or completely opened, so the cutting edges are not "cutting" you and your fellow occupants. If they cannot be removed, as much as possible, keep louvered windows and vertical blinds covered with curtains.

155. Electric stove or gas – get rid of the microwave.

Whether on a wood burning stove or over an open camp fire, wood fires are the most energizing method of cooking food. Unfortunately, they are also the least practical in modern dwellings. This makes gas cooking the best and most acceptable. Electric stoves are good enough, if you have no choice, but they do not radiate the food like wood or gas. Microwaves are not even to be considered as a means of cooking food. In fact, they do not cook food. What they actually do is essentially rearrange the molecules.

Radiant heat from wood or gas "energizes" food cooked by these means making the food more yang – which means more nourishing and vitalizing. Food prepared by a microwave remains yin, that is, weak and devitalized as the food never becomes energized. Microwave ovens also have the negative effect of fixing protein molecules, making them impossible to digest. Furthermore, the outside is not as hot as the inside of the item microwaved, which deceives the palate to eat and swallow that which can overheat the stomach lining. Over a period of time, these various shocks to the immune system puts the body into a pre-cancerous condition. While the lack of nutrition, even after a meal and though the body may feels full, results in a constant craving to eat in order to overcome the nutritional deficiencies that result from eating essentially lifeless food.

156. Fluorescent light fixtures.

Fluorescent light fixtures are another bane of modern design that can be held accountable for aggravating the psyche of many individuals especially in office buildings and other work places. Fluorescent lights present two problems: one, they flicker and hum incessantly and two, they usually lack the full spectrum of colors found in natural light. Being top heavy in yellow and the active colors, they over stimulate the

nervous system – "frying" the nervous system may be a more apt description.

Needless to say, in bedrooms, kitchens, or anywhere in the home that is frequently used, fluorescent lights with the continuous humming and flickering of the ballast with or without purple in the light output, results in individuals experiencing recurrent headaches, nervous irritability, shortened attention span, depression, and anti-social behavior.

Full spectrum bulbs are available in many hardware, health food, and lighting fixture stores. Even better is to remove these monsters of electronics and replace them with full-spectrum soft lighting provided by incandescent light fixtures. Ott lights are better and can also be obtained at most lighting fixture stores and are offered in many mail order catalogues.

157. Stairs without risers – "floating stairs."

Stairs without risers, which are usually found outside a dwelling as part of a porch, or leading you to a second floor landing, are sometimes found inside a home as well. This stairway construction is incomplete and allows the qi to "slip through the cracks" so to speak. The usual solution is to put a backing on these steps, install a runner carpet with a "meandering" design that flows from step-to-step or, if possible, to place some potted plants underneath to catch the qi and bring it back.

158. Thorny bushes or pointy-leaf plants.

Thorny bushes or pointy-leaf plants along pathways should be removed, or at least trimmed back as pointy-leaf plants are considered aggressive and hostile. Likewise, pointy-leaf plants near seating areas inside or outside of the house are perceived as uncomfortable, and under most circumstances, people will not sit near them. In similar manner, people do not feel comfortable walking along a path with thorny roses, cactus, or bougainvillea on either side reaching out to scratch their skin or tear at their clothing.

Peace

Things to Fix Immediately

Keeping the Home in Good Condition

Have nothing in your home
that you do not know to be useful
or believe to be beautiful.
~~ William Morris, artist & designer

Maintenance is of great importance in feng shui theory, as anything that is not right becomes a disturbance to one's inner sense of balance and distracting to one's focus. Any tension that undermines one's well-being, eventually upsets relationship harmony, distracts from one's ability to be creative and productive, and inevitably affects one's prosperity. These seemingly minor disruptions, if not kept in balance, when combined with an unexpected life upheaval then will require greater effort to overcome in one's attempt to again establish balance and equanimity.

I often think of the analogy of rolling a tire across an empty room. In all likelihood, the tire will hit the wall on the opposite side of the room. However, if there is one pencil on the floor in the tire's path, that tire will either roll over it or be slowed down by it, depending of course on the size and speed of the tire. If there are many small items in the tire's path, the tire has that many more obstacles to overcome. Again, depending on the size and speed of the tire, the tire will either overcome the obstacles or be eventually knocked off course.

In a similar manner, if we wake up in the morning and have to confront a series of obstacles, no matter how minor, such as a blank wall, a pile of books or laundry and other sundry clutter, squeeze by a sharp-pointed dresser and a towering armoire, by the time we get through the bathroom routine, get dressed, and are ready for breakfast, the psychological toll becomes quite heavy with our psyche and self-talk grumbling, and perhaps not silently.

If this is indicative of the pattern of the day, going to work on a crowded freeway and sitting in an office or place of business with equally as difficult feng shui, the breaking point is soon reached. Something has got to give, and it is always the weakest link, either emotional or physical. It is with this in mind that taking action to keep one's environment stress-free and harmonious is of the greatest importance. Use feng shui to identify and solve major problems, but don't neglect to keep basic maintenance in good order. Therefore, fixing that which needs fixing or adjusting feng shui cures that need adjusting, helps to maintain one's highest intention and continues to attract beneficial circumstances.

159. Leaky plumbing.

I find it interesting, how often I have observed that leaky plumbing or dripping faucets are the first thing mentioned in magazine articles introducing feng shui to the public. Money, also called "currency," flows like water, and leaky plumbing and dripping faucets are immediately experienced as loss of income or income coming in and "leaking" away. No water equates to no money, as when farm crops dry up in a drought. Good clean drinking water means good health and great abundance of life-giving qi.

160. Broken burner on the stove.

The cook stove is another symbol of prosperity that needs to be kept clean and in the best operating condition. If a burner is plugged or broken, money problems ensue. A broken burner on the stove also equals loss of money, as the ability to cook our food represents abundance as expressed by "cooking on all four burners." It is advisable to utilize all burners for cooking and not just favor one or two, as this comes to represent not taking advantage of all your opportunities and just limiting yourself to a few. We are truly blessed if we have a kitchen with a four burner stove, and not have to cook on Sterno, a camp stove, or a one burner hot plate. A five or even a six-burner stove is a sign of even greater good fortune.

161. Squeaking hinges, floorboards, or stairs.

Squeaking hinges or floorboards act upon the subconscious as a constant complaint. WD-40 the hinges or nail down the floor boards and your joints and other systems will flow smoothly and productively. There will be a lot less complaining about petty matters as well. Squeaky hinges always mean the people of the house are arguing. Loose or squeaky floorboards usually reflect feelings of uncertainty and insecurity.

162. Broken or cracked windows.

Broken or cracked windows can affect the eyes, as the windows are symbolically the "eyes of the house." To avoid eye problems, replace broken windows immediately. To see "clearly" with inspiration and with vision equals clean, unbroken windows. If you feel you are lacking in "vision," wash and clean your windows.

163. Stuck windows.

Stuck windows can affect career and or relationships by encouraging conflict and discord. Struggling to open a window or just not having that option, as with any frustration, resulting in complaining, with constant frustration invariably having a rippling effect through many areas of one's life.

164. Broken or cracked steps or concrete pathways.

Broken concrete or cracking and dilapidated steps, whether outside sidewalks, pathways, or driveways or leading up to porches, decks or side doors, all can indicate

problems with bones and joints. Whether it is stiff joints or a broken bone, keep all concrete, if not perfect visually, at least not dangerous or bothersome to walk along. If you have difficulty getting home, traversing dangerous and unstable broken wooden stairs, landings, or concrete walkways, it will also be difficult for good opportunities to come your way.

165. Install water filters.

Install water filters which remove chlorine, flouride, heavy metal contaminants, dirt particles, chemicals that have seeped into the ground water from agricultural pesticide/herbicide runoff, and in some areas parasites. Ideally, you want to filter all the house water. But at least install an under-the-sink filter or a counter-top filter for drinking and cooking water, and a chlorine removing filter on your shower head as the chlorine, and the resultant chloroform, mist in a shower is easily inhaled and, overtime, can be very toxic. There are also chlorine removing filters that hang from the bathtub faucet for running a chlorine-free bath.

Unfortunately, in the last few years many municipalities have started using chloramine (yellowish tinge), instead of just chlorine (greenish tinge), as a disinfectant. Essentially, chloramine is chlorine with ammonia added in order to make the chlorine more stable and evaporate slower. For chlorine removal a simple charcoal filter can be used. For chloramines, a more expensive catalytic filter needs to be installed.

It would be nice if civic municipalities would find saner solutions to protecting its citizens from polluted water, instead of exchanging one pollutant for another. Chlorine, chloramines, and the industrial waste used in fluoridation process as well as in toothpaste are just not beneficial for the human body. Notice the notification on toothpaste tubes that warn: "Do Not Swallow."

Longevity
Stylized Chinese Character

Change Your Location, Change Your Life

Global Feng Shui – Your Astro*Carto*Graphy® Map

(Reprinted from the Maui Special Edition #2 - Fall 1997 - Stress Free Living Issue)

———————————

166. Choosing the best geographical location for you and your family to live.

In the first issue of Maui Special Edition, I introduced you to some basic concepts of feng shui (füng sch'way), the art of placement and design. In this issue I would like to share with you an astrological technique that is similar to feng shui, and which I have been introducing to the feng shui community as Global Feng Shui. This technique is called Astro*Carto*Graphy. Where feng shui concerns itself with creating harmony in the immediate home environment by removing obstacles, moving furniture and use of color and symbols, Astro*Carto*Graphy concerns itself with which locations on planet Earth are most harmonious for you to live.

Many of you are familiar with some of the usual ways astrology can be used in self-discovery, understanding relationships and understanding the changes that happen throughout life (transits and progressions). An Astro*Carto*Graphy Map is a map of the world showing exactly where each planet was passing over at the moment of birth. Through my study of Astro*Carto*Graphy, I have found that different locations have different influences, making it easier or more difficult to manifest goals and even to resolve personality and health issues.

Whenever someone is considering a move to a new location, or is not happy where they are currently living, the Astro*Carto*Graphy Map helps to determine the best

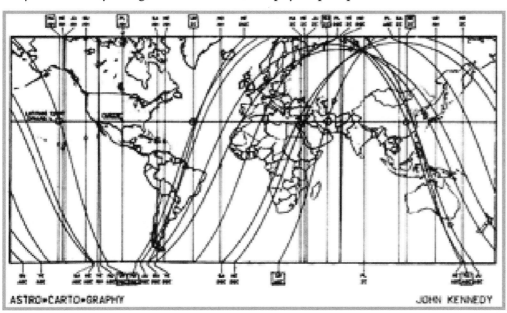

ASTRO*CARTO*GRAPHY   JOHN KENNEDY

location to move to. More frequently, I use this chart when an individual seems unhappy where they are, and there are no other astrological reasons to explain why life has been so tough for so long. In these situations, it usually turns out the individual is living on an unfavorable planetary line.

The planetary lines that are most favorable are Sun, Jupiter, Venus, and Mercury. Sometimes the Moon and Uranus are favorable especially when combined with the Sun, Jupiter, Venus or Mercury; never when next to each other or any of the more difficult planets. The lines that are most difficult are Saturn, Pluto, Mars, and usually Neptune, though I have known a few individuals to do well on that line as well. Though favorable lines seem most desirable, some people can use difficult lines to their advantage and sometimes difficult lines aren't as difficult when combined with a more favorable line. But most of the time, difficult lines reflect struggle in career, relationship and especially even health.

For example: a Saturn-line may be beneficial for a few years in helping someone bring structure into their life. But once they have their 'act together,' the best advice is, "leave." Living on a Saturn-line tends to be depressive, burdensome, alienating, lonely, frustrating, and contractive. Relationships tend to be characterized by rejection and abandonment issues, while health problems usually affect the bones, joints and or teeth.

Pluto-lines can be even worse. Pluto-lines may begin with a wonderful high, even ecstatic highs, but in short time the crest of the wave gives out, and there is a heavy fall. Again the advice is, "leave." Pluto-lines tend to affect health by undermining the immune system and by expressing deep core emotional issues as cancers and tumors, and other illness that "explode" from deep within the subconscious. On a Pluto-line, life is a continuous process of intense inner transformation and karmic cleansing.

Briefly, Mars-lines tend to be contentious, competitive and masculinizing in a negative sense. Head-strong Mars can give headaches and injuries. Uranus can be exciting, innovative and colorful, but often ends up as too erratic, nerve wracking, and unpredictable. Great for entrepreneurship and technology, but lacking in intimacy and commitment in relationships. Neptune, though creative, imaginative, idealistic and spiritual, tends to be nebulous, anxiety ridden, wishy-washy and rarely sees manifestation, with health issues being difficult and hard to diagnose. Both Uranus and Neptune may be more creative, spiritual or romantic when combined with a more favorable planet. The favorable planets bring creativity, popularity, positive relationships, feelings of well-being, and abundance.

So why would anyone choose anything less than the best planetary lines to live on? Karma, of course; the karmic necessity to work through specific lessons in life. Where

we live and choose to live fits our patterns. For an individual who has been struggling for years living on a difficult planetary line, looking at an Astro*Carto*Graphy Map usually means they are ready to make a conscious choice to live a more harmonious and fulfilling life.

Of course it should be understood that changing the feng shui of your home, or moving somewhere else on planet earth doesn't change your core issues. You always take yourself with you wherever you go. However, it should also be understood that by making changes on the physical, you set your intention to change on the spiritual. By moving furniture in your home or changing cities, you could remove additional frustrations in resolving these core issues sooner, rather than later. For example: an alcoholic in recovery may find more of an inclination to back-slide in certain locations and more support to grow and change in another.

It would be folly to think that just because you move to, or are living on your Venus-line, relationships will be easy, or you will finally meet your soul-mate. Indeed, if you still haven't resolved your core issues of a need to be in control, or your victim-victimizer issues, or whatever issues you have that have made relationships difficult in the past, you will still have them even on your Venus-line. You may even have a relationship that ends in divorce. However, compared to a Mars-line, even the divorce will proceed harmoniously, and you will at least part as friends. With the next relationship evolving even more joyously. Whereas on a Mars-line, the relationship is more likely to end in bitterness, and possibly with a difficult and bitter court room battle.

For people who travel from location to location there is another technique called Cyclo*Carto*Graphy. This is similar to a transit reading of the birth chart as it shows the changing energy. Former President Carter had Mars in Iran but it wasn't until Pluto went over Iran that this potential aggression exploded in the hostage controversy. Likewise, Pluto was transiting over Dallas at the time Kennedy was assassinated. For the rest of us mere mortals, the implications are the same. If you travel to a place during a poor transit, you are likely to experience some form of difficulty reflective of your core issues and evolutionary needs. I made the mistake once of traveling to an otherwise joyous Venus location when Saturn was transiting over head and found myself in a serious accident, which put me down for three days. And I was "lucky" (thanks to Venus, the primary influence in that area), it was not more serious than that.

Not all astrologers are experienced in Astro*Carto*Graphy Map interpretation, nor are the Maps generated on home computers as precise as the professionally plotted Maps by Astro Numeric Service. These finely produced Maps are 7 1/2" x 15 1/2" and are printed in color on quality paper. I have analyzed hundreds of Maps and can answer all your questions concerning where you presently live; or, if you are planning a move, I can help you choose a place that is best for you and your family.

145

Note to Revised 2012 Edition: Since this feng shui book was first printed in 2003, I have completed my next major book, *Evaluating Astro*Carto*Graphy Maps: Finding the Best Places to Live & Travel – Your Step by Step Guide.* This book with thirty-two color illustrations, case histories and sample interpretations is also designed with instructions easy enough for the layperson to follow, and who just wants to know what to do. The book comes with a one-hour companion DVD demonstrating the actual step-by-step instructions found in Chapters 8, 9 and 11.

For the student of astrology this book provides all the information needed to learn how to accurately evaluate Astro*Carto*Graphy Maps as taught by Jim Lewis, the originator of Astro*Carto*Graphy, in his Certification Course.

To order *Evaluating Astro*Carto*Graphy Maps:*
Finding the Best Places to Live & Travel – Your Step by Step Guide,
go to my web site: www.ElliotTanzer.com,
or if you are map challenged, or prefer professional assistance
evaluating your for Astro*Carto*Graphy Map, call me at: 310-281-6798.

Acknowledgment: The Astro*Carto*Graphy Map and Manual was developed by astrologer Jim Lewis to whose innovative and inventive Spirit we are greatly indebted.

Family

Exploring Other Ways to Feng Shui Your Home

*Feng Shui practitioners are artists and technicians of the ch'i flow,
using any means at their disposal to weave human and environmental ch'i
into patterns of nourishing energy, which feed and protect every part of your life.*

~~ David Daniel Kennedy, *Feng Shui Tips for a Better Life*

There are many other feng shui techniques in addition to the ones given in this book, all of which have great merit when applied properly. Unfortunately, some people have studied one tradition and, not having studied other systems, presume that their way is the best, the most powerful, and the only way to practice feng shui. It should be understood that whichever system you have invested years of study in will prove to be the most dynamic for you. However, being dynamic for you does not preclude that there might be other ways to accomplish the same positive goals.

I have had the good fortune to have studied with many teachers and have gleaned the best they have to offer. I have also had the opportunity to compare their variations. Some students see the contradictions in how different teachers interpret and apply the formulas as perplexing. They want a definitive system. A system without ambiguity. Feng shui as a life skill does not offer such a singular system.

Feng shui is a way of "seeing" the world, and a way of analyzing the energetics of a space. It developed over the millennium to meet the needs of different typographies and in the context of different cultural influences. Some of it is based on an individual's psychological response to the symbolism of the collective unconscious, and some feng shui evaluations are based on mathematical formulas. Some of it is intuitive and some of it is plain common sense.

Understandably, once you bring human sensibilities into any equation, there are going to be contradictions and variations. Rather than seeing differing interpretations and approaches as negating the validity of feng shui, I see the variations as liberating. I see the variations as an indication that there are many ways to solve a problem, and many ways to achieve an alignment that will bring opportunity for career success, good health, relationship harmony, and so forth.

It is also a way of understanding that if a problem cannot be solved in one system, perhaps a solution can be found in another. As it is unlikely to have 100% perfect feng shui with any system, each system we use adds to the total. Remember, the home is analogous to a container – a container with many holes leaking qi or energy. Our mission is to identify those energy leaks and then find ways to remedy the situation.

Landform School

Among the oldest traditional systems of feng shui is the Landform School, which it is believed originated in the mountainous regions of southern China. It is this analysis of how qi flows through the environment that is the foundation for all other feng shui approaches. Landform School analysis is the primary basis for the majority of the questions I have included on the Feng Shui Checklist. The basic level of Landform School Feng Shui is to analyze how qi flows to, through, and, around an environment.

After choosing your house based on the recommendations in this book, I encourage you to explore other systems, each of which will reveal subtler levels of qi flow evaluation. No doubt you will discover other problems to consider and be presented with other opportunities to apply feng shui principles and concepts. As no one gets a 100% good feng shui, with with good property location, siting of the dwelling, structural features, and how the room configuration you are already 80% of the way there. With additional adjustments using other techniques available, the feng shui of your home will grow stronger and you will enjoy greater success and harmony in your life.

Compass School Feng Shui

Essentially, the Compass School evaluates the influence of the magnetic field as determined by the eight directions of the compass divided into twenty-four subsectors. Two popular techniques from the Compass School are: Flying Star Feng Shui and Eight Mansion Feng Shui. The Flying Star system is one of the oldest approaches formulated in northern China. A Flying Star Chart is calculated based on the compass direction plus the construction date of the home corresponding to the 20-year cycle of Jupiter and Saturn. The derived chart becomes the birth chart, or "energy blueprint" of the home.

Experienced Flying Star practitioners can "read" the history of the home and its inhabitants from these charts. They can clearly determine health, relationship, and financial circumstances of anyone living in the home. Based on Annual and Monthly cycles, a trained practitioner can predict when good fortune or bad will likely occur. The first compasses were originally used by Chinese feng shui practitioners to determine the best direction for siting burial plots (Yin Feng Shui). The compass was later used by mariners to navigate the seas and by travelers to find their way across unfamiliar lands.

To study Flying Star Feng Shui can be quite daunting. Once the concepts are grasped and the formulas applied, the results can be quite rewarding. In my own struggle to learn this traditional form of feng shui, I devised three Master Formula Study Guides to put all the formulas at my finger tips, and a step-by-step Tutorial to make it easier for any student to learn . Ordering info can be found on my website: www.ElliotTanzer.com.

Eight Mansion Feng Shui

The Eight Mansion system also utilizes the directions of the compass to determine

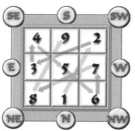

**Feng Shui Compass
with 24-Subsectors**

**Lo Shu Magic Square
with Path the Stars Fly**

**Sample Flying Star Chart
Period 6 – Subsector S1**

if the inhabitants are in harmony with a dwelling. Whereas Flying Star Feng Shui uses Five-Element Theory to harmonize a home, Eight Mansion Feng Shui uses an individual's birth year and gender to determine which compass directions bring the best energy. These directions are then used to determine whether you will have good fortune based on which way the top of your head is pointing when you sleep, which way you face when you sit at a desk, or as you walk out your front door.

Sometimes it may be suggested that an individual enter the home through a door other than the front door to tap into the best energy and insure success. Even which way the stove knobs are pointing, or which direction you have the rice cooker plugged into the wall can be used to evaluate if your food will be most nourishing. The location of a bathroom is also considered: will it flush away bad energies, or will it flush away good fortune?

Black Sect Tantric Buddhist Feng Shui

There is also a fusion of classic Chinese qi flow analysis with the altar building feng shui and transcendental techniques of the shamanic Bön tradition of Tibet. This system is called Black Sect Tantric Buddhist Feng Shui. This fusion of styles is the innovation of Grandmaster Prof. Thomas Lin Yun. It is this system that is primarily responsible for the emergence of feng shui into non-Chinese cultures since the mid-1980s. (The Bön is the spiritual and cultural traditions of the indigenous people of Tibet, which predate the influx of Buddhist teachings by several thousand years.)

It is the Black Sect use of the 3–Door Bagua (referred to on page 125) that is used in evaluating the Wealth and Partnership Areas of the home. The Black Sect tradition also places a strong emphasis on prayer (mantra), hand position (mudra) and visualization for setting intention. Prof. Lin Yun refers to the use of the orientation of the Bagua to the front door of the house as the Compass of the Heart approach.

[Note: This system was originally referred to as the Black Hat Sect. The term "Hat" has since been dropped to avoid confusion with the Black Hat Sect of the Tibetan Tantric Buddhist Kagyu lineage, whose titular head is His Holiness the Seventeenth Karmapa. I should also point out that, though developed among Buddhist, you do not have to be a Buddhist to use the Black Sect approach to feng shui.]

Regardless of which system is utilized, it is important to have a strong foundation as established by the feng shui solutions in this book. All teachers, regardless of which approach they have mastered agree, that without good Landforms, all other systems are less effective. Good Landforms are needed to activate the elemental interaction of Flying Stars, and are needed to support the good intentions of Black Sect remedies. With that in mind I encourage you to continue to explore the many dynamic levels of feng shui wisdom. May your life be blessed with good health and great good fortune.

EAST GROUP

Best Direction	Li FIRE	Xun WOOD	K'an WATER	Zhen WOOD
East	A	C	B	D
South	D	B	C	A
South East	B	D	A	C
North	C	A	D	B
Least Favorable Direction				
West	G	F	E	H
North West	H	E	F	G
North East	E	H	G	F
South West	F	G	H	E

WEST GROUP

Best Direction	Kun EARTH	Dui METAL	Gen EARTH	Qian METAL
West	B	D	C	A
North West	C	A	B	D
North East	A	C	D	B
South West	D	B	A	C
Least Favorable Direction				
East	E	H	F	G
South	F	G	E	H
South East	G	F	H	E
North	H	E	G	F

**Prof. Thomas Lin Yun
with hands in
"Blessing Mudra"**
4th International Feng Shui
Conference, Orland, Florida – 2001

My Recommendations:

You will notice sprinkled throughout the text of this book are inspirational quotes from many of the books listed in this Bibliography that help illustrate the principles and concepts of feng shui.

I have included these quotes because I felt the author had a perceptive way of verbalizing the situation being discussed. I hope these quotes will assist in clarification, simplification, or in some other way, in a nut shell, to assist you in understanding how feng shui actually works. I highly recommend each and everyone of these wonderful feng shui books.

An asterisk (*) indicates books that were especially important as sources for problems and or solutions. To these authors thanks, and thanks again.

Bibliography and Recommended Reading

Carus, Paul. *Chinese Astrology: Early Chinese Occultism*. LaSalle, IL: Open Court Paperback, 1974.
   (First published in 1907 as *Chinese Thought*.)

Coghill, Roger. *Electro Pollution: How to Protect Yourself Against It*. Wellingborough, England: Aquarian Press, 1990.

* Collins, Terah Kathryn. *The Western Guide to Feng Shui: Creating Balance, Harmony, and Prosperity in Your Environment*. Carlsbad, CA: Hay House, 1996.

* DeAmicis, Ralph & Lahni. *Feng Shui and the Tango in Twelve Easy Lessons*. Cuore Libre Publ., Bryn Athyn, PA: 2001.

Eberhard, Wolfram. *A Dictionary Of Chinese Symbols: Hidden Symbols in Chinese Life and Thought*. London: Routledge & Kegan Paul Ltd, 1986.

Eitel, Ernest J., *Feng-Shui: The Science of Sacred Landscape in Old China*. London: Synergetic Press, 1984.
   (First published in 1873 by Trübner & Co.)

* Fairchild, Denny. *Healing Homes: Feng Shui Here & Now*. Birmington, MI: WaveField Books, 1996.

Jofre, Michael J., and Robert T. McKusick. *Alive and Well: Neutralizing Environmental Radiations*. Globe, AZ: Biomagnetic Research, Inc., 1991.

* Kennedy, David Daniel. *Feng Shui Tips for a Better Life*. Pownal, VT: Storey Communication, 1998.

Kennedy, David Daniel. *Feng Shui for Dummies*. NY: Hungry Minds, Inc., 2001.

Kingston, Karen. *Creating Sacred Space with Feng Shui*. NY: Broadway Books, 1997.

Kwok, Man-Ho with Joanne O'Brien. *The Elements of Feng Shui*. NY: Barnes & Noble, 1991.

Lewis, Jim. *The Astro*Carto*Graphy Map Manual*. San Francisco: A*C*G, 1976.

* Lim, Prof. Dr. Jes T. *Feng Shui & Your Health: A Guide to High Vitality*. Singapore: Heian Internat'l, 1999.

* Lin, Jami - compiled & edited by. *The Feng Shui Anthology Contemporary Earth Design*. Miami: Earth Design Inc., 1997.

McKusick Charmion R. *In the Claws of the Dragon*. Globe, AZ: Biomagnetic Research, 1997.

Moore, Steve. *The Trigrams of Han: Inner Structures of the I Ching*. Wellingborough, England: Aquarian Press, 1989.

Ni, Hua Ching. *The Book of Changes & the Unchanging Truth*. Malibu, CA: Shrine of the Eternal Breath of Tao, 1983.

* Post, Stephen. *The Modern Book of Feng Shui: Vitality and Harmony for the Home and Office*. NY: Dell Publ., 1998.

* Rossbach, Sarah. *Interior Design with Feng Shui*. London: Penguin Arkana, 1987.

* SantoPietro, Nancy. *Feng Shui: Harmony by Design*. NY: Berkley Publishing Group, 1996.

SantoPietro, Nancy. *Feng Shui & Health: The Anatomy of a Home*. NY: Three Rivers Press, 2002.

* Skinner, Stephen. *Flying Star Feng Shui*. Boston: Tuttle Publishing, 2003.

* Skinner, Stephen. *The Living Earth Manual of Feng-Shui: Chinese Geomancy*. London: Penguin Arkana, 1982.

Swartwout, Dr. Glen. *Electromagnetic Pollution Solutions*. Hawaii: Aerai Publ., 1991.

Tanzer, Elliot Jay. *Exercises For the Spiritual Body*. Los Angeles: Self-Published, 1989.

Tanzer, Elliot Jay. *Evaluating Astro*Carto*Graphy Maps: Finding the Best Places to Live & Travel – Your Step by Step Guide*. Temecula, CA: Self-Published, 2010.

* Thompson, Angel. *Feng Shui: How to Achieve the Most Harmonious Arrangement of Your Home and Office*. NY: St. Martin's Griffen, 1996.

Too, Lillian. *Feng Shui Fundamentals: Wealth*. Boston: Element Books Ltd., 1997.

Too, Lillian. *Lillian Too's Personalized Feng Shui Tips*. Kuala Lumpur: Konsep Books, 1998.

Too, Lillian. *Practical Feng Shui: Symbols of Good Fortune*. Boston: Element Books Ltd., 2000.

Twicken, David, Ph.D, L.Ac. *"Flying Star" Feng Shui Made Easy*. Revised 3rd Edition. Lincoln, NE: Writers Club Press, 2000.

Twicken, David, Ph.D, L.Ac. *Treasures of Tao: Feng Shui - Chinese Astrology - Spiritual Qi Gong*. Lincoln, NE: Writers Club Press, 2002.

* Wong, Angi Ma. *Feng Shui Dos and Taboos: A Guide to What to Place and Where*. Palos Verdes, CA: Pacific Heritage Books, 2000.

Wong, Eva. Feng Shui: *The Ancient Wisdom Of Harmonious Living In Modern Times*. Boston: Shambhala Publ., 1996.

* Webster, Richard. *101 Feng Shui Tips for the Home*. St. Paul, MN: Llewelyan Publ., 1998.

* Wu, Dr. Baolin and Jessica Eckstein. *Lighting the Eye of the Dragon: Inner Secrets of Taoist Feng Shui*. NY: St. Martin's Press, 2000.

Wu, Wei. *A Tale of the I Ching: How the Book of Changes Began*. LA: Power Press, 1995.

* Wydra, Nancilee. *Feng Shui: The Book Of Cures*. Chicago: Contemporary Books, 1996.

* Yap, Joey. *Feng Shui for Home Buyers – Exterior*. Kuala Lumpur, Malaysia: JY Books Sdn. Bhd., 2006.

Yap, Joey. *Walking the Dragons with Joey Yap*. Astro TV Series (Episodes 1 to 8, English subtitles), 2009-2010.

Ziegler, Holly, MA. Ed. *Sell Your Home FASTER with Feng Shui: Ancient Wisdom to Expedite the Sale of Real Estate*. Arroyo Grand, CA: Dragon Chi Publ., 2001.

About the Author

ELLIOT JAY TANZER

Astrologer, Feng Shui Practitioner,
Writer and Teacher of Meditation and Metaphysics

Since 1973, Elliot Jay Tanzer has provided astrological services specializing in natal chart interpretations, future forecasts, relationship studies and Astro*Carto*Graphy Map analysis. From 1983 through 1989, after nine years living on the island of Maui, Elliot returned to Los Angeles and established an international reputation, while lecturing extensively at major expos, astrological conferences and metaphysical centers. He has also appeared on many radio and television shows. During these years, Elliot taught at Heartwood: California College of the Healing Arts and was awarded an Honorary M.A. in recognition of his many years of synthesis of Eastern, Western, and Hawaiian mystical traditions.

From 1990 to January 2000, Elliot again returned to Maui. During these years, Elliot immersed himself in the study of the ancient Chinese art and science of feng shui, published an alternative health and conscious living magazine, and continued to teach classes, and provide astrology readings primarily via the mail and recorded telephone consultations.

Since returning to southern California in 2000, Elliot continues to do presentations at expos, conferences and metaphysical centers. He is the co-founder the Integrative School of Feng Shui and is the designer of Master Formula Study Guides and other tools for feng shui practitioners. In addition to this book, *Feng Shui Secrets: Improving Health, Wealth & Relationship Harmony, featuring the Feng Shui Checklist*, Elliot's newest book, *Evaluating Astro*Carto*Graphy Maps®: Finding Your Best Places to Live & Travel – Your Step by Step Guide* (2010), with a one-hour companion DVD, continues Elliot's writing legacy of making complex subjects easy enough for the newcomer who just wants to know what to do, at the same time a training manual for the experienced practitioner.

Elliot's first book, *Exercises for the Spiritual Body: Meditation and Metaphysics – Their Practical Application (1982),* provides important insight into the nature of the esoteric anatomy, with guidelines for grounding, centering, chakra balancing, claiming one's psychic space, opening the Inner Eye of Seeing, often referred to as the Third Eye, and a technique for doing an aura brush down. There is a companion CD of the meditation described in the book. This Guided Visualization Meditation is excellent for anyone wanting to learn to meditate, or to help anyone in the healing or counseling professions, or who is psychically sensitive with a tendency to take on other people's energies. Check Elliot's website for recently released Guided Visualization Meditation CDs.

A complete list of lecture and workshop topics, an article archives, purchasing information
for various products and services and sign up for Elliot's newsletter can be found at Elliot's website:
www.ElliotTanzer.com.

To contact Elliot to order copies of any of Elliot's books, meditation CD, or feng shui tools,

by email: et@ElliotTanzer.com

by phone: 310-281-6798

or snail mail to:

Elliot Tanzer, P.O. Box 891924, Temecula, CA 92589

May you enjoy
a warm or cooling breeze.
according to your changing needs.

•

May you enjoy fresh flowing water
to nurture and refresh you.
so you may
enjoy good health.

•

May you have abundance.
enough to share with others.

•

May you enjoy
sweetness and harmony
in all your relationships.

•

May you enjoy a successful,
satisfying,
creative
and
peaceful
life.

•

May all sentient beings find peace and happiness
and the causes of happiness.

MAY PEACE PREVAIL ON EARTH